1953
MAKING A MARINE GRUNT WARRIOR

COLD WAR WARRIOR TRILOGY

1953
MAKING A MARINE GRUNT WARRIOR

DAVID D. FERMAN

Copyright © David D. Ferman.

All rights reserved. No part of this book may be reproduced in any form or by any electronic or mechanical means, including information storage and retrieval systems, without permission in writing from the publisher, except by reviewers, who may quote brief passages in a review.

ISBN: 978-1-64606-745-9   (Paperback Edition)
ISBN: 978-1-64606-746-6   (Hardcover Edition)
ISBN: 978-1-64606-744-2   (E-book Edition)

Every person that I wrote about in my Cold War Warrior Trilogy was, or hopefully still is a living woman or man. However, in my trilogy (*1953—Making A Marine Grunt Warrior, 1954—Making A Marine Pilot Warrior, 1955—VAH-7, Secret Navy Atom Bomber Squadron*), I changed the names of several persons in each book to avoid embarrassing them or their relatives. I owe those wonderful old rascals that much for being such good friends back then, and such great material for these three books now. Given all possible choices today, I would not and could not write these true stories in any other way.

These books are interesting, somewhat humorous and didactic because they are absolutely true. All of the events, places, attitudes and opinions are factual. It has been 64 years since 1955, so some other old duffer's memories may differ from mine.

Book Ordering Information

Phone Number: 347-901-4929 or 347-901-4920
Email: info@globalsummithouse.com
Global Summit House
www.globalsummithouse.com

Printed in the United States of America

TABLE OF CONTENTS

I. INTRODUCTION

1. SEA STORIES 1
2. COLD WAR WARRIOR TRILOGY 2
3. BACKSTORY 2
4. MOUNT FUJI NIGHTMARE 8
5. "OH MY WONDERFUL ONE, HOW I ADORE YOU." 9
6. KANSAS VS. MICHIGAN MARINE RECRUITS 10

II. UNITED STATES MARINE CORPS BOOT CAMP

1. MY FAVORITE U.S. MARINE CORPS QUOTE 12
2. FLOYD SNOW'S ROVING EYES 12
3. THE CHARGE OF THE POTBELLY STOVE 13
4. THE LESSON OF OL' GARBAGE MOUTH 14
5. "WHAT IS YOUR NAME…BOY?" 15
6. ADULT SUPERVISION 16
7. BOXING WAS NOT A SPORT FOR ME 17
8. "GUNG HO" MEANS "WORK TOGETHER" 19
9. EVERY MARINE IS A RIFLEMAN 19
10. PAIN HURTS 23

11. BIG AGONY AND LITTLE AGONY.. 25
12. AMBUSH AT TENT CAMP 25
13. MESS DUTY DELIGHTS.. 26
14. "I CAN'T HEAR YOU." 28
15. LUSCOUS LIPS GALORE 28
16. SEVENTY ONE HOUR FLU 30
17. "WHO IS LT.COL. STEVE CANYON?" 30
18. EVASION ALL NIGHT LONG 32
19. ALLIGATOR MOUTH/TADPOLE ASS 32
20. FIRST BAYONET TRAINING 33
21. U.S. MARINE CORPS HYMN 36
22. FIRST LIBERTY.. 38
23. U.S. MARINE QUOTE 39

III. DRILL INSTRUCTORS' SCHOOL

1. MASTER SARGEANT RAMSEY.. 40
2. GUNNY "SNAKE" WANTED ME GONE 42
3. LITTLE RED'S SKIVVIES 43
4. EVIL GENIUS... 46
5. FORM FOR SHELTER HALVES 46
6. FROM OCS TO FLIGHT TRAINING................................... 49
7. WHAT GOES AROUND COMES AROUND. 52
8. U.S. MARINE QUOTE 53

IV. JUNIOR DRILL INSTRUCTOR
WITH PLATOON 205

1. RECRUIT MALTREATMENT 54
2. "SIR. WHERE IS THE BEER, SIR?"...................................... 55
3. PVT. PARIS WAS TOUGH 56
4. PVT. JERRELES LITERALLY SHINED 57

5. THEY CAN'T KEEP BILL BRILL DOWN 57
6. "SIR. I AM BLIND, SIR." 58
7. "SIR. I JUST HAD AN EPILEPTIC FIT, SIR." 59
8. MAMA'S BOY 59
9. M1 THUMB: PRETTY DARNED DUMB 60
10. RECRUITS SNORE BY THE NUMBERS 61
11. ALL-AMERICAN PULLING GUARD WAS DISCHARGED ... 62
12. "HUTT, TWO, THREE, FIVE" (?) 63
13. POINTY RECRUIT BAYONETS 64
14. NOT LIKE JOHN WAYNE 65
15. PROFANE BAM DI 67
16. THE REVEREND RECRUIT 68
17. FATHER O'BRIAN'S BOMB BAY 69
18. "BUT WHEN THE CHAPLAIN GOES HOME…" 70
19. WORLD WAR II MOVIES 71
20. WEDDED BLISS: NOT IN MY BOOT CAMP 73
21. SGT. ARLEY DALE WRIGHT 73
22. C.I.D. SPOOK IN THE RANKS 76
23. AMMUNITION MANAGEMENT 76
24. POGY BAIT MARINES 78
25. U.S. MARINE QUOTE 80

V. MCRD CASUAL COMPANY

1. DEPOT LAMINATIONS 81
2. DEAR OL' MAUDE 82
3. INVOLUNTARY REFLEXES 83
4. BOB HOPE'S RANCH 84
5. ADVANCED COMBAT TRAINING 85
6. EVEN MORE IQ TESTING 86
7. FLIGHT PHYSICALS 88
8. FINALLY HOME SWEET HOME 90
9. U.S. MARINE QUOTE 92

VI. NAS MOFFETT FIELD

1. CPL. TILLERY 93
2. CLUE TO A LONG FOOTBALL SEASON 94
3. FORT ORD 95
4. PREMO NAVY CHOW 96
5. "PERMANENT PFC." ELADIO GONZALES 97
6. WELL-ARMED ROBBERY 99
7. GREEN MARINES 99
8. CPL. HOOKER 101
9. PING PONG CHAMPION 101
10. PFC. (LATER COLONEL) GEORGE BAILEY 102
11. UNPARALLED PLUPERFECT PRIDE 103
12. PFC. (LATER LT. COL.) JOE D. BOLLING 104
13. MASTER SGT. O'DAY 105
14. SGT. LEMAN BRIGHTMAN 105
15. COLD SHOWER TAP DANCE 107
16. SHE LED, I FOLLOWED. 107
17. WE LOST, I WON. 108
18. "SEA DADDY'S" VIP 110
19. PFC. CAVENAUGH'S NEAT MOM 110
20. THE INFAMOUS RATHSKELLER BAR 111
21. RHEA'S WRATH 112
22. LALA LAND 113
23. JUDY'S SCHOOL SONG 114
24. SIGGIES HANG TOGETHER. 115
25. SAN JOSE NIGHTS 116
26. PAY DAY PANIC 117
27. PFC. GEORGE JONES' PICKING AND SINGING 117
28. MOBILE MULTIPLE ROCKET LAUNCHERS 119
29. BOUNCY BALL HOOK SHOTS 121
30. "OH YES YOU WILL" 122
31. IT'S ALWAYS SOMETHING 124

32. SSGT REYES' BOXING LESSON 125
33. CPL. "FRENCHY" BESSIER 127
34. THE INFAMOUS PROPELLER CLUB 131
35. ENGLISH GRAMMAR CLASSES 132
36. ACCIDENTAL DISCHARGE 134
37. "HALT OR I WILL SHOOT YOU!" 136
38. PURPLE HEART 138
39. "AAA-GILE, MO-BILE AND HOS-TILE" 138
40. MARINE CORPS BIRTHDAY BASH 139
41. THE PERFECT PRISONER 141
42. USMC INSPECTOR GENERAL 143
43. POLICE UP THE BRASS 144
44. PFC. SNYDER 145
45. MEMORABLE MOMENTS 145
46. "THAT'S MEN'S WORK" 146
47. CHESTY PULLER'S JEEP DRIVER 148
48. SURPRISE, SURPRISE 150
49. THE NAKED TRUTH 151
50. THAT #$%&(@)+!! LENNY 152
51. SGT. BENNY 155
52. SGT. RECKLESS 156
53. COUSIN AMY HAD HER DOUBTS 157
54. SWEATING BULLETS 158
55. HARD TIME WAS NOT THAT HARD 159
56. A TOAST BY THE USMC COMMANDANT 159
57. PREAMBLE 160

APPENDIX

PREPARING FOR MARINE BOOT CAMP 161

LIST OF FIGURES

Figure 1. The Wichita Kansas Platoon 4

Figure 2. The Author Played Semi-Pro Baseball to
 Win Contracts with the Boston Red Sox............................6

Figure 3. Recruit Platoon 118, Day 3 in Boot Camp 15

Figure 4. Recruits Firing at the 500-Yard Line at Camp Mathews ...22

Figure 5. Marine Trained Rodent...34

Figure 6. Recruits Read Platoon 118 Graduation Certificates 37

Figure 7. Recruit Platoon 118 Graduation..37

Figure 8. Drill Instructors School, Class 19 Graduation 49

Figure 9. Recruit Platoon Final Inspection 77

Figure 10. Recruit Platoon Final Formation 77

I. INTRODUCTION

1. SEA STORIES

Some civilians and boot camp recruits may ask: "What the heck is a sea story?" An ancient and honorable tradition among the sea-going services, sea stories are true, usually first-person yarns about unusual and/or wondrous adventures such as grand and glorious victories, close calls, embarrassing faux pas, stupid mistakes, terrifying moments, dastardly deeds, galling disappointments, exotic locations, bawdy entertainment, hijinks usually when snockered, the women of (pick a place), "Dear John" letters and their often unforeseen consequences, commendations, awards, that 10 percent that never got the word, regrettable faux pas, interesting trivia, or anything else worth mentioning that happened during active or reserve duty in the U.S. Marine Corps, the U.S. Navy, the U.S. Coast Guard or allied sister sea-going services, usually at sea or across the sea, but not always

Sea stories come in a variety of sizes (a single paragraph or even a dozen or more typed, single-spaced pages), and a variety of contents such as those sea stories that typically:

a. Can usually be told comfortably in mixed adult company, including your mom, maiden aunt, and maybe even your bible-thumping pastor.

b. Are told among consenting adults, but probably not your mom or pastor, while leaving out very little adult content.
c. Are more appreciated by other salty old military personnel or veterans who were once, or will probably be in the same places or situations someday during his or her various tours of duty.

Have no fear, the sea stories in this book are a blend of all but category b, and are as true as memory, old documents and old photographs permit. So sit back, relax, read on and enjoy. You will not need a Thesaurus.

2. COLD WAR WARRIOR TRILOGY

This trilogy comprises three related collections of stand-alone sea stories in chronological order. These are: *1953–Making A Marine Grunt Warrior; 1954–Making A Marine Pilot Warrior;* and *1955–VAH-7, Secret Navy Atom Bomber Squadron.* These books are mini-memoirs and not day-to-day diaries. These sea stories are selected, generally short snippets that are often interspersed by days and even weeks on several occasions to avoid getting bogged down in boring, connective minutia.

3. BACKSTORY

Ever since I was eight years old in early1941, I wanted to be a United States Marine. Like nearly all of the other little whippersnappers in our low-rent, blue-collar, predominantly German-Irish neighborhood in Wichita, Kansas, we came naturally by our preference for the snazzy Marine dress-blue uniform and their well-earned reputation as fierce warriors.

During World War II, our government apparently did not trust our young men of German heritage to fight Hitler's Nazi Germany. Therefore, it seemed that every draft-age young man in our parish served our country in the U.S. Marine Corps and fought the Japanese in the Pacific Theatre of War whether they had volunteered for, or were initially drafted into the U.S. Army.

Until December 7, 1941—the day that the Japanese bombed our U.S. Navy Pacific Fleet at Pearl Harbor, Hawaii—the sermons at our St. Anthony's church were spoken in German. Additionally, the German/American Bund had been a formidable political movement of Nazi sympathizers in some other parts of America. Naturally, the U.S. Army had significant reservations about sending our young German-Irish guys to fight Nazi Germany even though everyone I knew in our diocese hated Adolph Hitler with an abiding passion.

Nine years later on 25 June 1950, the Korean War began when the 75,000-man North Korean communist army, equipped with a huge number of Russian T34 tanks, armored vehicles and top of the line MiG fighter aircraft invaded our ally South Korea. Two of my 18-year-old high-school friends who had previously joined our local Marine Reserve unit were immediately activated, and deployed to Korea. One was killed and the other was wounded and returned home to recuperate before our fall football season was history.

Hot to trot, I wanted to enlist in the Marines immediately after high school graduation—our neighborhood motto was "Don't get mad; get even"—but I was still recuperating from a football injury during my senior year so I could not enlist until November 1952. However, two supposedly sprained hands were discovered to actually be two broken hands—silly me—which further delayed my enlistment until February 1953 when 75 local studs (figure 1) enlisted in and around Wichita, Kansas to form Boot Camp Platoon 118 (otherwise known as the "Wichita Platoon") at the U.S. Marine Corps Recruit Depot in (MCRD) San Diego, California.

Figure 1. The Wichita Kansas Platoon

That whole rain dance began one day in late October of 1952 when I received a letter from my pal "Wild Bill" Brill, who had been our fullback in grade school, high school and the first year of college football. Bill and another good friend, Bobby Brady, had joined the Marine Corps the previous summer while I was working in the oil patch of southeastern Kansas to help pay for my sophomore semester's gas and beer tabs. If I had known their plans, I would have tried to enlist with them. Tragically, Bobby was killed during amphibious assault training near the southern California coast before he could be deployed to Korea. We Marines fight the way we train, and we train darned hard and very realistically so some accidents are expected.

After Bobby Brady's funeral, Bill was deployed to Korea with the First Marine Division. Months later, Bill wrote that he was fighting the North Koreans and Chinese hordes, and the Marines were kicking oriental butts left and right. He told me to hurry up and join the Marines before I would be too late to get in on that extremely exciting adventure.

At that time, I was playing football on an athletic scholarship at El Dorado Junior College (now Butler County Community College) and had earned a guaranteed football scholarship at Kansas State University for 1953 and 1954 so that I could realize my once-improbable ambition to earn a Bachelor of Science degree in petroleum geology.

On top of that neat deal, C. B. Masterson, the Kansas southeastern region's baseball scout for the Boston Red Sox gave me a second contract because of my two unusually good summers of Semi-Pro baseball after I opted out of their initial offer in 1951 (figure 2) after graduating from high school. Once again, I took that contract home, showed it to my family and friends, then I gave it back to Mr. Masterson a couple of days later. Naïvely, I really believed that I could always get another professional baseball contract either after I got out of the Marines or after I graduated from college. Like somebody quotable often said: "We get too soon old and too late smart."

In those days, any pay for play was a major "No No." If I had taken one thin dime for playing any sport, I would have lost both my existing football scholarship and my upcoming baseball/football scholarships. Although our Semi-Pro Baseball sponsor, Roscum Realtors payed most of the other key players on the team from $20 to an occasional $50 for each game (that was big money just to have fun playing baseball back in 1952) when we played in the National Semi-Pro Championships in Wichita. However, they paid me the approximate equivalent in six-packs of cold beer, which was apparently okay for some weird reason or other. Win or lose, we had some grand and gloriously raucous parties after many games and, because of those scholarships, I remained eligible to become the first in my family to earn a college degree. That lofty and formerly unlikely ambition beckoned me like the Sirens' songs from Homer's "Odyssey and Iliad."

Figure 2. The Author Played Semi-Pro Baseball to Win Contracts with the Boston Red Sox

By the way, a left-handed relief pitcher for the Boeing Aircraft Company's semi-pro baseball team—a former major league pitcher—was paid full union wages and benefits as a tool and dye specialist on the assembly line although he never worked a single day inside the Boeing plant. When called out on a fast ball pitch the first time I bated against that guy, I turned around and asked the home plate umpire if that pitch didn't "sound" a little bit low to him. Occasionally, that old lefty still had a heck of a fastball.

After another of my close friends was killed and several more were wounded in Korea, I bailed out of El Dorado Junior College (Juco) at the end of my sophomore football season and drove directly to the Wichita Post Office to enlist in the U.S. Marine Corps.

From the very first meeting, I got along great with the senior recruiter: Buck Sergeant (three stripes) Kuhn. Although the second smallest boy in my class from kindergarten through the eighth grade, by the time I played Juco football, I was 6 feet, 3 inches tall, weighed a solid 215 pounds (hint: eat a peanut butter and jelly sandwich and drink a big glass of whole milk every night just before going to bed), and qualified for a crack at Officer Candidate School after a tour in the war in Korea. The Marines seemed to like the cut of my jib, and I still lusted after that snazzy Marine dress-blue uniform. What red blooded American girl in her right mind could possibly resist that fan-danged-tastic uniform? My hope: not many.

So everything was moving along really well until Sgt. Kuhn asked if I was hurting anywhere. I was, so he sent me to a local doctor who X-rayed my right hand, which was broken when stomped in the second football game of the past season. Then, just for the heck of it, they X-rayed my left thumb that I broke when I hit the granite jaw of that plowboy who had stomped on my right hand. Old Doc Feelgood said that he was going to X-ray my head "because both of your hands are broken, you big dope."

Silly me, I thought that my hands were just sprained throughout the season because somehow I was sure that they would not work worth a flip if they were actually broken instead of just painfully sprained. Therefore, my plan to be in boot camp before Christmas and in Korea by Easter was put on hold. Looking back with 20/20 hindsight, I should have stayed in school until the end of the semester. Like some really smart guy often said: "We get too soon old and too late smart."

While waiting for my broken hands to heal, I stayed in contact with Sgt. Kuhn and swapped a few 10-cent beers on several occasions while he gave me tips about getting through boot camp. One of his best tips was: "Always answer every question truthfully, but never, never, never volunteer any additional information."

That little trick paid off big time when Sgt. Kuhn was filling out my medical questionnaire for me because both of my hands were still in plaster casts. When he got to the part about head injuries, he asked me if I had ever had a concussion. Truthfully, I told him that I was hit on the back of my head by a thrown baseball and had a concussion when I was a senior in high school. Then he asked me if that concussion ever bothered me. Truthfully, I told him that concussion did not bother me at all. Hell's bells, I had played two seasons of college varsity football as the first-string offensive/ defensive end on a championship team, two summers of semi-pro baseball at first base with a team-leading batting average, and since then was the club bouncer at the "54 Lounge;" a fairly rowdy "honkie-tonk" road house near El Dorado.

In my family, when we were injured, we were expected to deal with it, get over it, move on, and don't look back. At that time, despite my concussion, a more serious but unmentioned head injury and two broken hands, I firmly believed that I was in as good a physical shape as any, and far better than most.

The next obvious and dreaded question (at least obvious to me) had me holding my breath in anticipation. But Sgt. Kuhn did not ask me about other head injuries such as my six little cerebral brain hemorrhage blips in a row from a single injury caused by wearing a worthless plastic football helmet in 1950 at St. Mary's Cathedral high school. Our quarterback, Bob Walterscheid, also wore that same low-budget, worthless, pee-poor helmet, suffered the same darn injury that year, and was classified "4-F"; i.e., physically unfit for duty in the U.S. military.

Bottom line, I did not volunteer any additional information just like Sgt. Kuhn had told me to do. I was a fairly quick study back then. Then he changed the subject and asked me if I had broken any bones besides the ones in my plaster casts. A flood of relief washed over me as Sgt. Kuhn meticulously listed seven broken noses, three broken ribs and a broken foot. I would live my childhood dream: I would be a United States Marine.

4. MOUNT FUJI NIGHTMARE

While waiting for my broken hands to mend so that I could finally go to Marine boot camp, I had some unusual dreams that woke me up maybe a dozen times. In these dreams, I could clearly see a huge, snow-capped, volcanic mountain with a round symmetrical cone like Mount

Fuji in Japan. In each dream, the same loud, deep, precisely enunciating voice would thunder down from on high:"DAVID...FERMAN,.THIS..IS..WHERE..YOU..ARE..GOING...TO...DIEE!" Naturally, that shook my tree more than somewhat, but I did not let it change my plans. I decided that if I ever saw that darned mountain up close when I would be awake, I would do my level best to avoid the darned thing like the plague.

5. "OH MY WONDERFUL ONE, HOW I ADORE YOU."

After 70 of the original 78 of us Wichita Platoon volunteers passed our physicals (which showed that the recruiters back home were doing their jobs), and then raised our right hands to swear our allegiance to God, country and the U.S. Marine Corps, we discovered that guys under 21 years old could not buy adult beverages in Kansas City, Missouri. Okay, so most of us wandered across the bridge to Kansas City, Kansas where we could celebrate with pitcher after pitcher of 3.2 cold beer (think cold swill).

What we did was spend our first night as future Marines getting snockered in a grubby, run-down beer bar that would make the 54 Lounge outside of El Dorado or even the Silver Dollar Bar in north Wichita look like Sunday schools by comparison. That was one really rough, tough cantina, but just by the sheer force of our numbers, it was Marine recruit property until well after closing time.

There wasn't a dry eye in the whole bar when I played "Oh My Wonderful One, How I Adore You" on the Juke Box by the Gaylords about a dozen times, give or take a few, as each of us rookie recruits collected his own thoughts, hoped for the best, prepared for the worst, and ordered another pitcher of beer. The United States was at war in Korea, and the Marines, as usual, were the point of the American spear. Some of us would return to our families and loved ones in boxes, and others would undoubtedly be maimed for life. But all of us would face our enemies as U.S. Marines, the world's finest fighting machine, and that, we figured, was worth the gamble.

6. KANSAS VS. MICHIGAN MARINE RECRUITS

During World War II, Dutch Van Vessum's dad was a leader in the underground resistance against the Nazis in Holland. After the war, the Van Vessums moved to Wichita, Kansas. That's why my friend Dutch went to North High School in Wichita and played football there. I went to Cathedral High School and played against him. That was enough reason for him and me to eventually tussle with each other on the train to boot camp. But since neither of us could whip the other in the cramped confines of the convertible sleeper chairs, after about ten minutes of tussling and rolling around without making any progress, he and I called a truce and joined forces to take on about eight of our guys who were playing tackle football in the train's oversized restroom car just ahead of us.

Of course, we had bitten off more than we could chew, so Dutch and I were losing that epic potty skirmish until Jerry Hutchinson, a large, fun-loving lineman also from North High School, joined in on our side, and we finally threw everyone else out of the restroom and gleefully claimed it as our prize possession.

That was fun, but we were still looking for a bit more excitement. So the whole Wichita Platoon headed for the next sleeper car behind us, which was full of Marine recruits from Michigan. Lucky for them, they heard us planning our raid as they walked through our sleeper car, and quickly barricaded the door to their car with their luggage so that only one of us at a time could breach their door; and that guy would get pummeled from all sides until he retreated.

That siege lasted on and off again for almost two days. In fact, five reserve Navy Shore Patrol (SP) guys came aboard the train at Salt Lake City to ruin our fun. However, all 70 of us ganged up on them, gleefully tossed them back off the train again with not too many bruises, and we had a grand and glorious time while it lasted. As Marine recruits, we were not ready to take orders from a bunch of reserve sailors. What Marine would ever admit any joehootinanny disgrace like that? Not a single one of us junior Jayhawks would ever consider allowing that shame to descend upon us.

For some reason, the local cops did not show up until the train pulled out of the station. Somehow, we had the distinct impression that the Salt Lake City Police Department did not think much of their local Navy reserve SP guys. However, when the train finally arrived in Los Angeles the next day, a squad of Marine Military Police (MPs) boarded the train, kicked butts, took names and re-established absolute order. Both the Kansas and the Michigan recruits were darned well cowed by the time that train rolled into San Diego. Those Marine MPs did not fool around. We knew that they would gladly put a hurting on all of us if we gave them the least excuse.

Like a wise man once told me: "Good judgment comes from experience, and a lot of that comes from bad judgment.

II. UNITED STATES MARINE CORPS BOOT CAMP

1. MY FAVORITE U.S. MARINE CORPS QUOTE

"Some people spend an entire lifetime wondering if they made a difference. Marines don't have that problem."

Ronald Reagan
President of the United States of America

2. FLOYD SNOW'S ROVING EYES

When we were temporarily billeted in the receiving barracks during our first two days as Marine recruits, the Drill Instructors (DIs) in charge of that barracks did their best (or worst) to change our cheap civilian crap ways. The first thing they did was line us up indoors in three squads at attention, and told us to find a spot on the bulkhead (*i.e., the wall*) straight ahead, lock our eyes onto that spot and keep them that way. Then they began their loud, profane orientation tirades, which distracted recruit Private (Pvt,) Floyd Snow (my good buddy who was later killed at the Pickle Meadow winter training camp after his one-year tour of duty in Korea) to move his eyes off his chosen spot on the bulkhead. That was a heck of a "No No." So the DI grabbed this very large Indian guy and threw him against the bulkhead. However, although I was a "good guy" recruit and had not moved my eyes off my chosen spot on the bulkhead, I made the mistake of standing between Floyd and the bulkhead. I paid for that mistake as I was slammed against that bulkhead three times by Floyd's big body each time Floyd lost track of his spot on the bulkhead.

Long story short, I was pretty well pounded to a pulp. However, Floyd was doing just fine as I absorbed his every impact meant for that darned bulkhead. In fact, that rascal was enjoying the excitement while I was paying the price for his darned entertainment. That's how I learned that come rain, flood, poop or blood, ol' Floyd could resist just about anything except temptation; just like me.

3. THE CHARGE OF THE POTBELLY STOVE

Later, after that same DI ran us ragged because we could not get outside the Receiving Barracks and into formation fast enough to suit him, one of our guys saw that DI slyly lock the front door from the outside. So when he blew his whistle for us to assemble outside again, Floyd, Dutch and two other former football players from Wichita North High School grabbed an old fashioned, iron, potbellied stove in the middle of the room and used it as a battering ram as they ran through the door with it sliding ahead of them on the floor.

That bodacious trick broke the door off its hinges and knocked the clock-watching DI off the small porch and onto the sidewalk. We were all lined up in formation before that DI could get sorted out and, since nobody knew who had used the stove as a battering ram and destroyed government property, we all suffered the consequences until long into the dark of night. After lights out, in total darkness, several anonymous recruits were heard crying themselves to sleep.

Welcome to the U.S. Marine Corps. We had volunteered, so we had no grounds for complaints. Some of us understood that. Some did not.

4. THE LESSON OF OL' GARBAGE MOUTH

As I said before, our recruit platoon was comprised of 70 guys from Kansas (mostly from Wichita), four short, squat Italian kids from Michigan who looked like identical peas in a pod, and a 27-year old, former Army guy and certifiable twit from back east who could not say three words without one of them being the "f" word. None of us guys from Kansas could stand that boring, repetitive potty mouth, and we avoided him even after he was erroneously designated the platoon Right Guide just because he was quite a bit older than the rest of us, and had previously been in the Army. Normally, Right Guide is a position of honor; but not in our platoon.

Since this blowhard was 27 years old and the little Italian guys were all 17 or 18 years old, they followed him around like the pied piper throughout boot camp, the rifle range at Camp Mathews and advanced combat training at Camp Pendleton before being deployed to Korea.

According to my pal Dutch Van Vessum, on their first day in Korea, our platoon was moving in a spread-out formation toward our main Line of Resistance (MLR) when they came under intense North Korean/Chinese heavy artillery fire. Ol' Garbage mouth immed-iately jumped into a still-smoking artillery shell crater—which should have been the safest place since artillery shells almost never impact in the exact same place—the four little Italian Marines jumped in behind him, followed by another ChiCom 152mm artillery shell that instantly killed all five. What are the odds of two artillery rounds hitting in the exact same spot? Considering cannon recoil and other dynamics on the battlefield, those odds must have been several million to one.

The morale of this story: I'm not sure, but there must be one in there someplace. Maybe it is something about our former Platoon Right Guide saying God's name in vain again and again and again without letup. They say that when called, our Lord will eventually answer you in a variety of ways. None of us were surprised when we heard about that ironic tragedy.

5. "WHAT IS YOUR NAME...BOY?"

All Marines take a 30-inch step at 90 steps per minute when marching, and 120 steps per minute when double-timing (jogging) formation to get from point "A" to point "B." No more, no less, no latitude allowed. The stride and steps per minute are exact. There is no room for deviation. "One heel, one heel" the DI chants as 75 boot heels hit the ground simultaneously as one (figure 3). A good DI turns the cadence and commands into something like a synchronized guttural song so that the cadence is always precisely the same. "Hareep per yer leoft, yer leoft-right-a'-leoft."

Figure 3. Recruit Platoon 118, Day 3 in Boot Camp

All marching commands are divided into two parts: the preparatory command and the command of execution. A two-step pause comes between the preparatory command and the command of execution so that the recruits or actual Marines will always start, pivot, halt or perform another marching movement on the proper foot at the exact same time. "To the rear"...step...step... "Harch"... step...step...pivot ...etc. In my experience, the DI's accent is always southern whether he is from Dallas, Texas, or Bangor, Maine. Throughout boot camp, the platoon's DIs are each "Mr. Marine Corps" to the recruits; a teacher to look up to. The DI is a fair but rough and hard-charging teacher who can be intimidating and almost God-like to his platoon; even to Fish Eaters like me and Hard Shell Southern Baptist recruits like the majority of our platoon.

A two-year, first team letterman on a championship college football team, a bit bigger, a bit older and a lot better prepared thanks to Sgt. Kuhn's advice back in Wichita, I was relatively more comfortable in boot camp than the average Marine recruit, and confident that I would do okay if I would just hang in there. However, one morning the whole platoon messed up miserably while learning the manual of arms with our newly issued M1 rifles, so we were catching unrelenting hell from our DI, as was only right. Then suddenly, although I was about three inches taller than him, one of the DIs grabbed me by my buttoned dungaree collars and jerked me down to his size so that we were nose to nose. From that proximity, I saw his bulging eyes glaring into mine; his flushed, angry, tight-jawed face, and smell his morning coffee and stale cigarettes on his breath that was washing over me.

I had not previously been singled out for individual attention that intense, close and personnel. So I braced myself as he bellowed: "What… is…your…name, BOY?" My heart pounding like a washing machine full of five-buckle overshoes, I barked back: "Sir. The private's name is…" My mind raced double time then turned into mush. I could not remember my own name; neither first nor last name. Thankfully, I knew that it was stenciled on my bucket back in our Quonset hut. Therefore, I figured that I would be prepared the next time a DI would single me out.

I was back in my grove, until I remembered that my name was also stenciled on my chest right above my dungaree pocket. Was I intimidated by that DI? You damn betcha' I was intimidated out of my cotton-picking mind, and I don't mind admitting it.

6. ADULT SUPERVISION

Since they patched us up in the field and in battle, Marines often call Navy corpsmen our "adult supervision." However, in boot camp I called them something else. The Navy corpsman in the Marine Corps Recruit Depot (MCRD) dentist's office took great delight in asking each new Marine recruit if he was tough. When I answered that I was indeed tough enough, the corpsman prepared me for drilling a cavity in my tooth without any antiseptic to deaden the pain caused by the drill. After that first such rain dance, I never again returned to a military dentist's office, which may have been the sneaky method behind their pain-filled game. Who knows? Anyway, that unforgettable example certainly worked on me.

7. BOXING WAS NOT A SPORT FOR ME

After about four or five weeks into boot camp, I was ordered to box this very big but still bacon-wrapped mama's boy from a competition platoon. That was quite a surprise to me. I had not anticipated having to box with anybody. Although normally comfortable in a boxing ring, I was a bit concerned that one lucky, really hard punch on my previously injured head without a protective helmet might tumble my gimbals. But there was no way out without a medical discharge, so I decided to get very serious very quickly and deck that guy before he could possibly get lucky and accidently ring my bell. So I went after him like it was a life-or-death brawl rather than just another minor cog in our boot camp training regimen.

However, when I hit his hard head with my right jab, which was encased in a marginal boxing glove, my previously injured right hand was suddenly racked with so much throbbing pain that it was basically useless. So I hit him square on his nose as hard as I could with my best left-hand uppercut, and he sat down on the deck *(i.e., the floor)* as my left thumb began pulsing in pain clear up to my elbow. Bad news. I knew that I could not throw another good punch that day, so with two and a half rounds to go in the bout, instead of going to a neutral corner, I stood directly over him, bended down and told him quietly through clenched jaws: "If you get up, you sorry #$%&@#, I'm gonna' bust your #$%&*$# face."

Fortunately for me, that young recruit took my bluff as seriously as it was intended, and he stayed seated on the deck until the DI counted to ten. Otherwise, with neither of my hands in any condition to hit anything, kick boxing would have been introduced to the USMC curriculum right then and there. For crying out loud, I was not going to lose to that chubby puss gut if I had to head butt him or bite him into submission. But most important of all, I was not about to let our DIs know how much my hands were hurting at that moment. Those guys would have sent me to sickbay and I could have been set back a week which would separate me from my pals in the Wichita Platoon.

The problem with winning a boxing match in the Marines was that one way or another, as long as I was winning, I had to keep fighting in various platoon competitions. If I would intentionally lose a fight to get the heck out of that loop, I thought that maybe I could get my bell accidently rung and possibly even get my mental pots and pans scrambled more than somewhat. I really didn't know, so my only logical choice was to keep winning really short boxing matches without getting my bell rung even once. So that's what I did, with many thanks to the several right-handed guys who had never fought a left-hander before, and could not figure out a left-handed boxer in just three two-minute bouts.

The secret as a left hander in the boxing ring is to keep jabbing my right hand into my opponent's face while moving to my right so that a right hander had to keep constantly moving to his right. That way, most right-handed guys can't jab straight ahead worth a hoot, and he would have to awkwardly cross his best stuff, his right hand, over his left jab, which is not the way to win a boxing match.

When I talked with my opponents after each boxing match, none of them had ever put on the boxing gloves with a lefty before. That was a wonderful, almost unfair advantage for me, and I gladly took advantage of it every time I crawled in a boxing ring. I won all but one fight in the first round, and I won that one in the second round because that opponent was fairly tall and stayed away from me for the first two-minute round while I figured him out.

Like I mentioned before, those recruits were boxing because their DIs told them to box, while I was boxing to put them down quickly to avoid any chance of another concussion or worse. That made a hell of a difference. Fortunately, I never had to box against another left hander. I'm not sure how that would work for me. Thank goodness, I never had to find out.

Talking about head injuries, I thought that even many "littles" can often make a "much." Whatever that could be, I did not need another "much" right then.

8. "GUNG HO" MEANS "WORK TOGETHER"

During the 20-mile hike to Camp Mathews in full field gear, one of our recruits coughed up quite a bit of blood from a long-forgotten foreign object that had been lodged in his lungs for many years since he was a kid. At least that was his story. However, this recruit was totally Gung Ho, so he did not want to drop out of our formation for fear of being discharged from the Corps. Before the march was over, I was carrying both his M1 rifle and mine slung over both shoulders, another recruit was carrying his field marching pack over his own pack, a third was carrying his 782 web gear with canteen and first aid kit slung over his shoulder like a Mexican bandito in a low-budget western movie, and two more guys were literally helping him walk.

Until a sick recruit actually dropped out on his own volition, our DI's would not make him get into the meat wagon that trailed our platoon by about half a mile. However, immediately after we triumphantly marched through the main gate at Camp Mathews in good order and looking sharp ("Lift your head and hold it high, 118 is passing by"), one of our DI's took the hurting, exhausted but proud recruit to the camp sick bay. We never saw him again, and he was eventually given a medical discharge. That was one determined young Marine recruit.

It is too darned bad that we could not keep him around if only for inspiration.

9. EVERY MARINE IS A RIFLEMAN

"This is my rifle. There are many others like it, but this one is mine." Every Marine is a rifleman. Whether Grunt Mud Marine, belly robbing cook, cannon cocker, tank jockey, office pinkie, grease monkey, fly boy air crew, sea-going bellhop or whatever, every Marine—whether male or female (i.e., a "BAM")—is first and foremost a certified, qualified rifleman. As succinctly summarized by General A.M. Gray, Commandant, USMC: "All other conditions are secondary." Uuuu-rahhh!

By the way, that is one of the major differences between the U.S. Marine Corps and the U.S. Army. When you have a reinforced Army infantry division on line, you normally have about 2,500 trigger pullers or so out of something like12,000 to 14,000 soldiers. Everyone else is in support of the 2,500 trigger pullers. However, with a Marine division on line, especially in an unusual condition like when the 1st Marine Division was surrounded by three Chinese infantry divisions at the Chosin Reservoir, you get about 12,000 trigger pullers who are all good shooters and can't wait to get a good sight picture on the Bad Guys.

Another difference, the Army's philosophy is massed fires sprayed all over the place, while the Marine philosophy is directed fire; i.e. one aimed shot, one enemy casualty. We're funny that way. Every Marine rifleman carried ten clips, each clip holds eight rounds of M1 rifle ammunition in the pockets of his 782 web gear. Do the math. That's the reason why the 1st Marine Division decimated the three ChiCom divisions that were specifically tasked to destroy the 1st Marine Division.

Basic rifle and pistol training and qualification as well as hand grenade and machine gun orientation were conducted at Camp Mathews, which was a permanent tent camp high in the California hills (the local folks call them "mountains" but that's a joke). Only the chow halls, recruit showers, sick bay, main crapper and the administration pogues were located in wooden buildings.

The normal rifle qualification syllabus was exactly three weeks long. The first week was dedicated to snapping-in with the M1 rifle to perfect the three primary, steady firing postures: offhand standing, sitting and prone. A major effort each day was dedicated to learning to steady the M1 rifle for better accuracy in each posture with the aid of an adjustable leather sling. Done correctly, the recruit can learn to aim his rifle rock-solid steady on target when aiming in any posture. I learned to love my rifle sling, and used much of my meager spare time working with the brass adjustment hooks so that I could quickly and easily adjust my sling to whichever firing posture was needed at whichever range. An all-purpose "hasty sling" in the field was a little faster and almost as good for all three postures, but not quite good enough for best results when qualifying with the M1 rifle at Camp Mathews.

Just as important were acquiring and holding a proper sight picture, breathing techniques to help hold the rifle and sight picture steady (while acquiring a target, take a breath then breathe out half of that breath), squeeze rather than jerk the trigger, then look for the next target.

The second week at Camp Mathews was principally dedicated to developing everything learned in Week Number 1 to begin live firing at the progressive distances of 200 yards (standing off-hand posture), 300 yards (sitting posture with knee support), and 500 yards (prone posture). Rifle coaches spread out to give recruits personal attention: one dedicated rifle coach for each two or sometimes three recruits. A recruit pit crew moved the targets up and down to mark the shooter's accuracy after each practice shot except for rapid-fire shooting. Elevation and crosswind adjustments were carefully recorded in each recruit's rifle log book and his sights were adjusted on his own rifle. Proficiency was extremely important. Accuracy was essential.

At that time, every Marine recruit was required to shoot right-handed for qualification unless he had a release note from an eye doctor that verified that the recruit's right eye was not the best for accurate shooting. That was the only way a recruit could be allowed to shoot left-handed. Of course, that was a major problem for me. I am left-handed, my left eye is my overwhelmingly dominant eye, and my left foot kicks extra points, field goals and punts good enough to get me the essential scholarships necessary to go to college free gratis.

Basically, my right hand was essentially along mostly for the ride. However, I could not declare that my right eye was not up to accurate shooting right-handed because I was a budding OCS candidate and OCS candidates could not have a weak right eyeball. I was screwed. I had to shoot right-handed for qualification. That was the pits. Hunting back home, I shot rabbits in the head while they were running fast and erratically over bumpy plowed fields, but I had a bad feeling about right-handed shooting from the start.

The final week was split between timed firing for M1 rifle qualification and working the targets in the butts to pinpoint the other recruit shooters' scores in real time. Unfortunately, our final qualification day was anything but perfect. On that sloppy day, the wind was a significant factor, blowing from our left to right. That had only a minor effect on a bullet at 200 yards, and a bit more at 300 yards. Nevertheless, I was shooting fairly solidly in the sharpshooter category until we moved back to the 500-yard line (figure 4) where the crosswind had a far greater effect because it was blowing erratically in gusts on each bullet for a longer time. I had no data in my rifle log to adjust precisely to each of those variations. So my Camp Mathews rifle coach and I guessed at the crosswind effects (we call that "Kentucky windage"). We guessed wrong and I slipped back into the top of the Marksman category, missing Sharpshooter by only one shot from 500 yards.

I was devastated. I knew that I should, and later I would re-qualify as a Sharpshooter with the M1 rifle, and later with the .45-caliber Colt model 1911 pistol. In fact, years later in 2003 at age 70, I fired a 246 score out of a possible 250 with somebody else's 9mm Glock pistol to qualify for my Texas conceal-and-carry license. But that day at Camp Mathews with so much on the line, I was devastated when I did not qualify at least as a rifle Sharpshooter.

Figure 4. Recruits Firing at the 500-Yard Line at Camp Mathews

Of course, I was not the only recruit ambushed by that fickle crosswind. Some of the recruits in our platoon who had been shooting Expert dropped down into the Sharpshooter category. A couple of our recruits did not qualify, and were set back a week to another platoon to try again. That was no consolation to me. As a rabbit slayer on the plains of Kansas where I shot running jack- and bunny rabbits with a .22-calibre Marlin lever action rifle, I always put meat on the table. So when I arrived at the Camp Mathews, I was fairly confident that I would shoot Expert, and then I might go on to become a Marine sniper. As my Dad always said: "Anything worth doing is worth doing well." Ergo, if you are going to be a rifleman, be the best darned rifleman you can be, and that would be a sniper.

However, I did not know that I would be forced to shoot right-handed and right-eyed with iron sights at 500 yards with a booger of a crosswind in the air. So I had to revert to Plan B: to go ahead and get with the OCS Program at Quantico, Virginia. Sometimes you have to suck it up and work with what you can get. I knew that I could re-qualify at the Quantico rifle range, and then I would have both. Every path has a few mud puddles along the way. Mine was no exception.

In war, each Marine must be able to shoot accurately no matter what the weather. I got a taste of that at the 500-yard range at Camp Mathews.

10. PAIN HURTS

One of the traditional recruit-on-recruit dirty tricks at the rifle range was when the "salty" recruits who had already qualified on the firing line passed the word to newly arrived platoons to look out because their DIs and rifle coaches were sure to pull a dirty trick on them just for fun. Of course, that happened to our platoon during the week when we were "snapping in" to learn the Marine way ("the only way") to fire offhand while standing, sitting on the ground and laying prone in exactly the right postures for proper rifle support and accuracy. Shooting a rifle in the Marines is not only an art, but also a discipline. No trigger jerking is allowed. Mess up once and you would find a kindly mentor whispering friendly advice in your ear. Mess up twice and you would find a DI or rifle coach sitting on your back or else nose-to-nose where he would discuss your genealogy and addled mindedness at the top of his lungs. Every recruit dreaded a third foul up. You talk about hell on earth.

After the first full week of snapping in, a recruit could easily be convinced that his DIs and rifle coaches would gladly do him physical harm as an instructional example. That was the best time to pass the word to future shooters that when they first fire their rifles, they should not snuggle that metal rifle butt up tight against their shoulders as instructed because that was just a nasty trick that the DIs and rifle coaches used to hurt the recruits' shoulders as a lesson not to be forgotten.

Invariably some of the recruits in the newest platoon would act like they were going to snuggle their rifles tight against their shoulders when firing, but just before the first command to "commence firing" was given, they would slyly move the rifle butt about an inch away from their shoulders so the rifle recoil supposedly would not hurt the recruit nearly as much as snuggling it tightly against their shoulders. City boys who have never fired a big-bore rifle are usually the most susceptible to that hogwash.

Therefore, at that first shot the 30-06 caliber M1 rifle's recoil would slam the metal butt plate against the shooter's shoulder. That would hurt more than somewhat and usually leave a mark. That was when the new guys would know that they had been had. Additionally, the DIs and rifle coaches could then see clear evidence of which recruits were listening to their lectures and trusted their mentors, and which recruits obviously did not. Of course, after traditional tricks like that, the DIs and rifle coaches always knew in advance that would happen so they were ready and waiting to rain all over any recruit who was dumb enough to show that he was nursing a bruised, very sore shoulder.

Which reminds me of Roy Clark's country/western classic song: "If I Had To Do It All Over Again, I'd Do It All Over You" cha, cha, cha.

11. BIG AGONY AND LITTLE AGONY

As part of the exercise routine at Camp Mathews, our DIs would duck walk us (squat down and scoot along like a duck) and otherwise exercise us in platoon formation up and down two fairly large hills appropriately called "Big Agony" and "Little Agony." Late one evening while the platoon was duck-walking after dark, I accidently tripped over something and rolled into a ditch near the top of Big Agony, but nobody noticed as I lay there in the dark untangling my legs and nursing a heck of a cramp as the platoon disappeared over the hill without me. However, I just hunkered down and relaxed for a few minutes because I knew I was between the platoon and our tent camp where we were bivouacked that night. They had to come back to where I was laying, so it would have been stupid to try to get up to catch up.

In a few minutes, when the platoon returned over the hill while still duck walking, I popped back into formation unnoticed and finished the drill comparably well rested. A couple of nights later the same thing happened again, but that time on purpose. I had so much company in that darned ditch that we had to give it up because the DIs were sure to notice the depleted ranks mo skoshi. Occasionally, there is no strength in numbers.

Later, when I became a DI, I always stayed on the ditch side of the platoon on Big Agony, and carried an issue flashlight so that no boot recruit in my platoon could sneak an unauthorized break like I had enjoyed so many months before. Like they say: "Live and learn."

12. AMBUSH AT TENT CAMP

One dark evening just about a week before we graduated from tent camp, one of our temporary DIs called the right guide and squad leaders into the duty tent and told us that we were a number of buckets, yard brooms, rakes, etc. short of our required complement at Camp Mathews. Then he mentioned that a nearby platoon would be returning to MCRD the next morning, so that could be a good place to find a few things that we needed. He did not need to say any more. We knew what to do.

As we handpicked our raiding party, that same DI slipped over to the targeted platoon and told one of their DIs that we would be coming after lights out. So when our 10-man raiding party arrived to fast finger what we needed, it seemed like their entire 75-man platoon jumped us, a serious free-for-all broke out between the tents in moonlit semi-darkness, we were losing big time, and had to hotfoot it out of there mo skoshi.

Back at our tent camp and licking our wounds, we then picked two 100-yard-dash track stars from Wichita North High School to sprint through the other platoon's tent camp yelling like banshees, grab anything that they could snatch off the broom and rake racks, and keep running in the other direction away from our platoon. Then they would toss their ill-gotten bootie all over the dark field as diversions for the chasers to hunt in the dark. Of course, our track stars snuck back to our camp by a different route.

As planned, almost the entire competition platoon chased them over the hill and into even deeper darkness, so that the rest of our platoon in the second wave were able to walk in unchallenged and take everything that we needed from their equipment racks. We then hid their stuff and our stuff under our tents where no one could find them without a fight, tripled the night watch, and slept in our dungarees and boondocker boots just in case those guys figured who we were and then wanted to mess with us again.

At calisthenics before breakfast the next morning, that same temporary DI congratulated us for our ingenuity. We would have cheerfully strung him up and disked him on the firing line just for drill. Some of us were really hurting, but we would not let him know it. Although a few of us were festering more than somewhat, at least we did not have any sucking chest wounds.

Like they say: "Sometimes you have to give some to get some."

13. MESS DUTY DELIGHTS

When we served our one week of mess duty at the main recruit chow hall back at MCRD San Diego, most of our platoon peeled potatoes, mucked around with the garbage cans, swamped out serving tubs, handed out food on the hot line, and cleaned the chow hall fore and aft before and after three meals each day. Somehow, I was assigned to hand out the white mess-crew uniforms. I didn't ask for that pud job, but I was mui tickled to pull that light duty for the whole cotton-picking week. It gave me a lot of free time to check-out what was stored where, and how the overall system worked. With the huge amount of food that was served each day, the accounting system for side dishes and sandwiches was not worth boo doodly squat. If we couldn't play with those cards, we might as well fold our tents and walk away hungry.

We had an average of 22 recruits in each of three Quonset huts, with the DI's duty hut jammed into more than one half of a fourth Quonset hut. The recruits in each Quonset were responsible for fast fingering their own snacks and hiding them with their gear under their bunks. The guys in our Quonset decided to keep it simple. We went for sandwich fixings: loaves of fresh bread, sticks of real butter, jars of peanut butter and jelly, and nothing else.

Immediately after lights out, in total darkness, all 22 of us broke out our stashes on the bare cement deck at the rear of our Quonset and made crude but really tasty sandwiches. However, a funny thing happened. Every night for seven nights in a row, when Dutch Van Vessum would reach for the bread and butter, some stealthy rascal, undetected in the total darkness, smeared Dutch's bare leg with a stick of butter; again and again and again, but only his leg. And every time, Dutch would cuss in a loud whisper so that the DI in the next Quonset would not hear his muffled protest, grab for the unseen culprit, come up empty handed, grab for the unseen bread, and get his leg buttered again.

For the entire week, that quiet, lurking, diabolical, see-in-total-darkness culprit was never detected, and his name has remained a mystery to this day. Thank goodness, my buddy Dutch did not catch that culprit and get really mad; but that was one time that he did not get even. However, now it can be told. Hey good buddy, that sneaky, diabolical, bad-nasty culprit was your old wrong-handed, good looking, squad leader and pal: me.

14. "I CAN'T HEAR YOU."

I don't remember the reason, but I needed to talk to the duty DI about something that could not wait. So I walked over to his Quonset hut office and knocked on the door. As always, the DI yelled that he could not hear me. So naturally, I knocked on the door a heck of a lot harder, but still got the same "I can't HEAR you" response. Since my knuckles were already sore from the first two iterations, I pounded the heck out of that door with the bottom and better padded parts of my fists, but darned if he didn't bellow again: "I CAN'T HEAR YOU, BOY."

Well hell, those were my best shots with my fists, so I kicked the bejabbers out of that door three or four times as the racket reverberated throughout that Quonset hut and I probably did some damage to the DI's door as well.

Then I heard: "What the HECK, Who IS that?" followed by "GET IN HERE!" I knew that he was sitting behind his desk, and I could get out of sight before he could open his damaged door, so I did. "Sayonara, Sir, I'll talk to you some other time."

Funny thing, every boot recruit in Platoon 118 heard that bodaciously loud hammering on the DI's door, but somehow nobody saw who the heck kicked the dickens out of the DI's door. That's how we all got extra PT with our M1 rifles, and an extra field day cleaning and inspection after the DIs dumped over all of our racks and the sand-filled fire buckets all over the deck as well.

That's some of the reason why I owed those guys a lot more than just the money I lost playing poker during the two-day railroad trip from Kansas City to San Diego. At that time, except for our potty mouthed Right Guide, Platoon 118 was indeed our family.

Who'da thunk it only a few weeks earlier? Not me.

15. LUSCOUS LIPS GALORE

After about eight weeks in boot camp, a few of us potential OCS candidates were given a second IQ test unannounced and unexpected. We were pulled off the steamy drill field all hot, tired and sweaty, then herded into a fairly warm room that was cooled only by the onshore breezes blowing through open windows. Think pop quiz in algebra right after a really hard, sweaty, varsity football game.

Our main monitor was a young female officer who was all business, although she still looked awfully good to me; especially since I had not seen a woman in about 10 weeks. She was, in a word, gorgeous. However, IQ tests are serious business in the Marines, and I took them very seriously. As was my habit with timed tests, on the first pass I hurried through the whole test and answered as many of the questions that I knew for sure. It would be terrible if I timed out without completing all of the easier questions. Then, I went back through the test to pick up the harder questions that would take a little more time to calculate. In fact, there was one question that I did not understand at all, so I raised my hand for the beautiful lady (BAM) officer to come to my desk and explain the question so that I could at least take a wild shot at answering it.

When she leaned down to whisper so that we would not distract the other recruits being tested, she tumbled my gimbals. Looking up at her, all that I could see was that she had the reddest, most perfectly shaped, kissable lips that I had seen in a very long time. She smelled awfully good too. As she explained the intent of the puzzling question, I sat there staring at her lips, mesmerized, and lost in some kind of euphoria. The fact is, I did not hear one single word that she said. To me, she was just humming melodically

After she walked away, I realized that if I ever met her again, even in a telephone booth, I would not be able to recognize her face. You talk about tunnel vision. So I took a wild guess at the answer and moved on to the next question. My recess fantasy was over. It was time to get back to work and do the heavy lifting. Fortunately, a whole bunch of my wild guesses were somehow on target, so that I did very well. Boy, was I ever surprised after wasting all of that time. I picked up something like seven or eight points which did me a lot of good later downstream

16. SEVENTY ONE HOUR FLU

Right after my second IQ test, I got the flu so bad that right after I reported to the base sickbay, I passed out. Then, the next day when I finally woke up, the Navy corpsman on duty in that ward demanded that I get up eee-mediately if not sooner and make my bunk as if preparing for an inspection. Later, I learned that I would be set back one full week to another platoon after 72 hours in sickbay.

At the 71-hour mark, I put on my dungarees and boondocker boots and walked back to my platoon without being released for duty. When I arrived back at my platoon, I had the distinct impression that my Senior DI had been counting the hours and did not think that he would ever see my smiling face again. So I smiled a lot, but for some reason, he did not smile back.

17. "WHO IS LT.COL. STEVE CANYON?"

One fine afternoon, totally unexpectedly after I had stood a midnight-to-0400 fire watch, a couple of other recruits and me in Platoon 118 were pulled out of ranks and marched double time to the MCRD Administration Building. As we arrived, we were told that we were about to have our OCS interviews with senior Marine officers, so we had better get squared away and stand by to stand by. Apparently, the review panel wanted to see how well we reacted to stress while on our feet.

Sitting at a long table were several full-bull colonels and several half-colonels, all of whom wore snazzy dress khaki uniforms adorned with lots of colorful campaign ribbons, commendations and shooting medals. I'm not sure of the exact numbers because I was blinded by all of that brass in one place and somewhat overwhelmed by the occasion. Aside from the movies, I had never seen that much brass in one place and I was darned well impressed. Actually, "apprehensive" would be a better word. No, make that "gut-wrenching shook up and out of my tree." Yeah, that's more like it.

I cannot remember where I was in that rotation. I think that I was one of the first to be questioned, but that did not matter. Anyway, the first question from the panel of very serious Marine officers was: "Who is Lieutenant Colonel Steven B. Canyon?" Say what? Astounded, I replied that Lt.Col. Steven B. Canyon is a comic strip character illustrated by Milton Caniff, and an extension of the 1930s comic strip "Terry and the Pirates." My Dad had been the editorial cartoonist on the Wichita Beacon Newspaper for more than 20 years. A newspaper family, we not only delivered newspapers to our neighbors and other customers on our paper routes, but we read the daily newspaper from front to back including the comics and the want ads. Apparently the brass had done their homework on me.

The second question was no less amazing. I expected them to ask me to recite the Marine General Orders, or possibly list all of the detail parts of the M1 rifle and the exact order in which they were assembled or disassembled. I could do that. But the second question from that illustrious panel of senior warriors was as surprising as the first. "What is the difference between 'slanted journalism' and 'biased journalism'?" Thank goodness that sweet old Sister Mel Essa had been our journalism teacher in high school where Sally Carney and I—with a little help from a couple of talented sophomores—had won All-American, All-Catholic and the Quill & Scroll awards for our school newspaper in our junior year. Therefore, I had that question down pat and delivered a too-long tutorial on the subject essentially chapter and verse.

By that time, I was really pumped up. What would they ask next? My heart was pounding like a Gene Kruppa tom tom drum solo, but I would be darned if I would let them know it. To my absolute surprise, the next question never happened. I was excused to snap to attention, do a sharp about face, leave the room and return to my platoon. I had been accepted to the fast track to OCS. I did not think that was as good as being a Marine sniper, but sometimes you have to work with what you have.

Gung ho. Semper fi. Thank you, Jesus, Mary and hoooooly St Joseph.

18. EVASION ALL NIGHT LONG

Just before the end of boot camp, my senior DI informed me that I was missing one dungaree battle jacket and one pair of dungaree trousers, and that another platoon was doing their laundry that night. Of course, I knew what was expected and I prepared as best I could. When ready, my face was as dark as Sammy Davis Jr's.

After lights out, I crawled on my belly more than 200 yards over the nearly-flat sandy beach. When the wash-line guard turned to watch an aircraft carrier entering the harbor in the moonlight, I grabbed a battle jacket and trousers, and then crawled 200-plus yards back to the potty Quonset hut where I discovered the worst of all possible foul-ups: that battle jacket had three stripes on it.

So I crawled back 200 plus yards, bid my time until the new wash-rack guard turned his back, threw the DI's jacket onto the laundry line, grabbed another one my size that had no stripes, and crawled back over the sandy beach again just in time for reveille. That darned rain dance had taken the entire night. That morning at inspection, one of our DIs complemented my determination and ingenuity, but I was too darned worn-out to give a flip. I would have been glad to just buy a new battle jacket, but that was not the Marine recruit way at that time.

That was also the day that our senior DI called out the entire platoon on the drill grinder and announced: "We need 75 volunteers to give blood. Aten…hutt. Left…face. Forward…march."

19. ALLIGATOR MOUTH/TADPOLE ASS

A recruit I'll call Pvt. Schmidt was a fairly tall, fairly muscular recruit who picked a fight with me for no good reason that I could understand. I think it had something to do with me being a squad leader, and he had some kind of a beef about that. Heck fire, if he really wanted to be the danged squad leader, I would have gladly given it to him or anyone else. Life would have been a lot less complicated with someone between me, that garbage-mouthed Right Guide, and our four DIs.

Schmidt and I were about the same size, but I really did not want to fight him during boot camp unless absolutely necessary. I already had enough bubblegum on my plate. But then his alligator mouth overloaded his tadpole ass, and he came at me with fire in his eyes. Since I did not want to get another concussion or worse, I got real serious really quickly and dropped him with two quick shots to his big, soon flattened snot locker that bled like the dickens all over his battle jacket and boondockers. Later that same night while I was on the 8 p.m. to midnight fire watch, I found him squatting in the dark behind the latrine Quonset hut. He was still holding a bloody handkerchief to his nose and mumbling over and over like a mantra: "They ain't gonna' break me. They ain't gonna' break me."

Like the General Orders specified, I had to report Pvt. Schmidt's situation to the duty DI, who told a couple of recruits to take Pvt. Schmidt to the sick bay on the other side of the parade grinder where they reported that Schmidt had dropped a locker box on his nose; twice. A general consensus among our squad, we thought that he must have had other irons in the fire beyond a broken nose because we never saw him again. I definitely would not want a hot head like him jerking on my foot to wake me up some dark night for a midnight fire watch. The duty fire watch carries a really big, nasty club until relieved of his duty.

20. FIRST BAYONET TRAINING

The bayonet is the Marines' quintessential weapon. As stated in the *Navy Times,* November 1994: "Marines know how to use their bayonets. Army bayonets may as well be paper-weights." When running low on ammo and/or in close quarters combat, Marines are famous for killing our country's enemies with our bayonets. We never hesitate to "fix bayonets." The Japanese had the reputation as fearsome masters of Jujitsu and all of those oriental martial arts, but whenever they tangled with the Marines man-to-man, face-to-face in World War II, the Marines almost always won the battle. So much for much of that martial arts superiority hogwash (figure 5).

Our senior bayonet instructor was a large, intense, imposing African-American Marine Sgt. who taught bayonet fighting techniques by the numbers, and then followed up with lightning fast, cat-like balance and precision to demonstrate the tricks of the trade.

Figure 5. Marine Trained Rodent

We had heard that he had actually killed a half dozen Chinese and/or North Koreans in a series of desperate fights at the famous battles at the Frozen Chosin Reservoir where the First Marine Division faced three Chinese divisions and decimated all three that were specifically assigned to destroy the "Fighting First." To watch that Marine's spring-loaded lethality, you would think that his weapon of choice was a razor-sharp Marine bayonet. Maybe it was.

As recruits, we closely watched his every move and worked hard to copy his techniques as well as his intensity. When he slammed the dummy with a powerful vertical butt stroke from his M1 rifle, the mechanical target shook so violently that we expected the darned thing to fall to the ground. His long thrust buried his bayonet to the hilt as his characteristic growl echoed throughout the platoon. Face to face, that Marine was the last person an enemy would see on this earth. He was truly inspirational. I could not wait for my chance to show my mastery of an iconic Marine weapon: the bayonet.

As I started my turn on the bayonet course, I was all pumped up to show our illustrious instructor what I had just learned. As I approached the first dummy, I stopped head-on straight away, downward slashed with my bayonet, and delivered a devastating vertical butt stroke with everything I had in it. Actually, what I did was to break my wooden M1 rifle stock cleanly into two pieces. I was all pumped up, but done for the day. After that, I was a lonely spectator while the rest of my platoon polished their techniques and had a heck of a confidence-building workout with a true bayonet master.

So what now? We had a drill-field inspection the next morning with our competition platoon. Our senior DI did not want me to sit out that event. Then, just after evening chow, my senior DI called me into his duty hut and presented me with another rifle that looked like it had been lost on Okinawa during WWII and had just been found the day before he issued it to me. It was in deplorable condition from the rough, stained wooden stock to the gnarly trigger housing group and grungy barrel. I must have looked pretty stupefied because my DI assured me that this miserable wreckage would be ready for inspection the next morning. All I had to do was just get to work and stay with it until that rifle gleamed like new and worked just as smoothly as every other rifle in the platoon.

Long story short, after lights out, me and my decrepit, old (but new to me) M1 rifle spent most of the night in the potty Quonset hut as I salvaged as many parts from my broken rifle (i.e., the trigger housing group, butt plate, cleaning kit, etc.), disassembled and cleaned every detail metal part with steel wool and then applied a light coat of oil. I sanded out the imperfections in the wooden stock, then rubbed, stained and sealed it. Then I reassembled the rifle, re-oiled it and rubbed it down some more. Amazingly, the previously grungy looking barrel bore looked like it was about an eight out of ten condition (pretty darned decent considering where I started) after I was finished reconditioning it. Who'da ever thunk it? Not me, that's for sure. If I would have had the tools to salvage my original barrel. I would have had a nine out of ten.

About 04:30, a little before reveille, I finally hit the sack fully clothed in my dungarees without even removing my boondocker boots. It seemed like only seconds later that the bugler blew reveille and I was splashing water on my face, shaving with my eyes at half mast, and moving out for morning calisthenics before marching down to the belly robbers for what they laughingly referred to as breakfast ("shit on a shingle" and all of the coffee that I could beg or borrow). Later, while all of the other recruits were giving their rifles a final cleaning before inspection, I changed into a clean, fresh set of dungarees and was standing tall when the senior Charley Company DI inspected both platoons.

Just before I was inspected, I noticed out the corner of my eye that our senior platoon DI whispered something to the senior company DI, who then stepped in front of me and took my rifle with one fast, rifle-popping motion. Maybe it was just me, but it seemed like his inspection of me and my rifle took about twice as long as any of the other inspections including a couple of yard apes who got gigged. Then, he returned my rifle with a full, 360-degree (propeller-like) rifle rotation around the balance point that ended with a resounding slap on the rifle stock that could be heard anywhere on that huge drill field. I had passed muster, but without hardly any sleep in the previous 28 hours, and I still had about 14 hours to go before blessed lights-out again. Like the song says: "One step at a time, boy. Just one step at a time."

Do you think that maybe my friend Sgt. Kuhn back in Wichita had sugar-coated some of his boot camp memoirs? Would a good friend do that to a naïve young friend? Nahhhhhh! Not unless he had yet to meet his monthly recruit quota.

21. U.S. MARINE CORPS HYMN

I loved the Marine Corps Hymn from the first time I heard it played when I was a kid. The Hymn was made for marching. After I graduated from boot camp and became a full-fledged U.S. Marine (figures 6 and 7), I stood a bit taller and marched more proudly every time I heard it; especially when played by a full orchestra or large marching band with lots of thundering tympani. As a matter of fact, I don't think the words could be said any better. See what you think.

Figure 6. Recruits Read Platoon 118 Graduation Certificates
(From left to right: Pfc's. William Ramirez, Gerald Casey, Erwin Littrell, Dave Ferman, and Floyd Snow)

Figure 7. Recruit Platoon 118 Graduation

"From the Halls of Montezuma to the shores of Tripoli.
We will fight our country's battles in the air, on land and sea.
First to fight for right and freedom, and to keep our honor clean,
We are proud to claim the title of United States Marines.

"Our flag's unfurled to every breeze from dawn to setting sun,
We have fought in every clime and place where we could take a gun.
In the snows of far off northern lands, and in sunny tropic scenes,
You will find us always on the job, the United States Marines.

"Here's health to you and to our Corps, which we are proud to serve,
In many a strife we've fought for life and never lost our nerve.
If the Army and the Navy ever look on Heaven's scenes,
They will find the streets are guarded by United States Marines."

Semper fi.

22. FIRST LIBERTY

On our first liberty in San Diego after 12 weeks of boot camp, we were thrown out of every bar in the downtown area. Despite our civilian clothes, our high and tight haircuts and Marine cordovan shoes gave us away. So we were carded and ejected from every bar because none of us was 21 years old. We could not buy an adult beverage although most of us were on the fast track to Korea where the chances of getting killed, wounded or mutilated were pretty darned high.

Then, the sky opened and we saw our former Number Four drill instructor (I will call him Sgt. Newton) directly across the street. I explained to the other guys that they had better cool it because Sgt. Newton was mine. Any one of them could have his turn later, but since we had taken 12 weeks of him, I really wanted to know now if he could take five minutes of me. I wanted him badly. Again, many "littles" had made a "much" and that much was an uncommon opportunity that could not be wasted because it might not happen again.

However, when we caught up with him, we discovered that Sgt. Newton was big buddies with the bartenders who operated the Carousel Bar and had kicked us out earlier that evening. But surprise, surprise; Sgt. Newton bought several rounds of mixed drinks for all five of us with no questions asked from the formerly uncooperative bartenders.

Then, out of the kindness of his big and tender heart (say what?), Sgt. Newton volunteered to take all of us to Tijuana, Mexico, just over the border in his large Chevy station wagon. Once there, we had all of the Mexican alcohol that a young Marine could drink ("Jose Cuervo, you are a friend of mine, cha, cha, cha") and still stand somewhat upright. When we were inevitably all flat broke, one of Tijuana's infamous teenaged cops was seriously considering throwing all of us in the town hooskow for public intoxication when our new best buddy and former DI reached down into his sox and found a $20 bill, slipped it under the table to the junior cop, and we escaped back across the border before that cop could change his mind.

Bottom line: we never did find out if our former DI could take five minutes of me or any one of the other newly minted Marines. Like they say: "the best laid plans of mice and newly minted U.S. Marines are sometimes led astray."

23. U.S. MARINE QUOTE

"The deadliest weapon in the world is a Marine and his rifle."

General John "Black Jack" Pershing, Commanding General in Europe, U.S. Army, World War I

III. DRILL INSTRUCTORS' SCHOOL

1. MASTER SARGEANT RAMSEY

Just before we graduated from boot camp and became real U.S. Marines, we received the official word that the Officers' Candidate School (OCS) at Quantico was unexpectedly overloaded with a bow wave of graduating college Naval ROTC seniors. Therefore, we enlisted Marines could not begin our OCS training until at least the spring of 1954. Not only that, but instead of going right into advanced combat training at Camp Pendleton, two of us would go directly into DI School at MCRD San Diego. That was a huge surprise because until then, all DI school candidates had to be combat veterans and NCOs: i.e., noncommissioned officers; at least corporals.

We were neither, and I was convinced that I did not belong in DI School by any way you could look at it. In fact, I believed that I did not have the chance of a snowball in Hell of graduating from DI School. But orders were orders, so I had to salute, say "Aye aye, Sir (i.e., "I hear you and will obey you, Sir") and take my best shot at an extremely unlikely goal.

Although just six weeks long, DI school was considered to be one of the most difficult schools in the Marine Corps. Over half of every class of highly vetted, combat-proven candidates with OCS IQs (120 and above) had eventually washed out or dropped out along the way. All DI candidates had to be in excellent physical condition to keep up with the constant overall fast pace, and to pass the continuous, accelerated physical challenges. He had to be a pretty darned good student in the classroom to pass the daily scheduled and pop written and oral tests, to essentially memorize the "Landing Party Manual" (the 2-inch thick comprehensive guidebook of all things Marine), and to be a leader on and off the drill field. I was in a heap of trouble and I knew it. To my knowledge, this experiment had never been tried before in the U.S. Marine Corps.

Fortunately, we had an extra week to study the Landing Party Manual, run the various obstacle courses, and get into even better shape before 60 to 70 DI candidates were finally assembled to begin the formal training of DI School Class 19. That week of preparation, in addition to the regular formal training, was the key for me to hang tough and finally graduate. During that constant running, calisthenics, unit maneuvers and bookwork, I went into downtown San Diego just once on a quickie liberty. After striking out at every bar downtown, I was sorry that I wasted my time.

Another reason why I didn't go on liberty was that first I had to pass inspection by Master Sergeant Ramsey, the most squared-away Marine I have ever seen and may ever see. MSgt. Ramsey sat at attention at his desk on only one butt cheek at a time so as to keep from wrinkling the military creases in his trousers or those in his blouse (i.e., shirt) either. His shoes were always spit-shined to a high gloss. His brass belt buckle was highly polished on both sides. He went home to his wife every day at noon to change into a newly cleaned and properly ironed uniform. A Marine's Marine, MSgt. Ramsey had picked up a couple of purple hearts in Korea on top of a couple during WWII because he zigged when he should have zagged.

Best of all, he won the silver star medal by destroying not one but three North Korean T-34 tanks with an old WWII bazooka while the South Korean and American armies were collapsing into the Pusan Perimeter on the southern-most tip of Korea. Then, the newly arrived Marine Regimental Fire Team sharpshooters began picking off the North Korean infantry that should maneuver with the tanks as their eyes and ears. So the North Koreans decided to send their tanks into battle with no supporting infantry troops. That way, the bad guys had no external eyes and ears to guide them. That was a disastrous mistake.

The heavy armor on the front and sides of the Korean T-34 tanks could not be penetrated by our old WWII bazookas, so MSgt. Ramsey laid in a ditch high in the mountains on the main road south to Pusan until each tank passed him. With no supporting enemy infantry to bother him, he then got up and blasted each tank in their unprotected engine compartments at their rear ends. That blew them all to hell one by one. One such kill was heroic; but three tank kills to block and then backup the North Korean Army's advance through a mountain pass into Pusan was incredible. Those heroics should have rated the Congressional Medal of Honor or at least the Navy Cross.

I really admired MSgt. Ramsey, and eventually we became good friends. Thank goodness for that because his second in command hated my guts with a burning, unwavering passion. A gunnery sergeant, that top level instructor was dedicated to ensure that I would fail the course.

2. GUNNY "SNAKE" WANTED ME GONE

Gunnery Sgt. (I forgot his name after so many years) was also a highly decorated veteran from WWII and Korea. He was a squared-away Marine, knew his business like the pro he was, and he looked like a poster Marine; that is, he did until he spoke. On line in combat for something like 18 months in Korea with Colonel Chesty Puller and the 1st Marine Brigade of the "Fighting First" Division, he must have suffered from battle fatigue, shell shock or something nasty like that because when he spoke, he would involuntarily shoot the tip of his tongue out between his lips and then snap it back into his mouth like a snake.

From my first day in DI school, Gunny Sgt. Snake did not like me one little bit, but I don't blame him. First and foremost, I was not qualified according to the old rules. Maybe it was also because he thought that I laughed a lot during calisthenics while others were sucking air and/or dropping out, especially when only mad dogs and Irishmen should go out in the noonday sun. What Gunny did not know was that when pushed to my physical limits, I grunt a lot and make a chuckling sound rather than whine while sucking air. But what the heck, I had quite an advantage. I was a two-year college football letterman who had just graduated from 12 weeks of physically challenging boot camp. Many of my new classmates were wounded Korean War vets who were recently released from various hospitals to return to active duty, but were not quite up to the rigors of continuous mental stress as well as the physical challenges and calisthenics of DI School. Each of those Marine warriors wanted to be a DI, and each of them had definitely earned the right to try.

Maybe Gunny Snake thought that a candidate who was grinning and chuckling a lot on the side was a dummy and did not belong in his prestigious DI school. Or more than likely, he may have heard that I secretly called him Gunny Sgt. Snake, and he was not pleased. I do not know his exact motive, but every day and in every way, he was determined to kick my donkey out of his school. He certainly had a big advantage, and I was definitely the underdog in that contest.

That was fuzzy bug time. Like they say back in Kansas: "When all has turned to clabber, eat a fuzzy bug the first thing in the morning, and your day just has to get better."

3. LITTLE RED'S SKIVVIES

Even after all of these years, I could not forget the surprised, utterly bewildered look on Gunny Sgt. Snake's face when I aced the classroom written work (all of which was graded on a curve so some of the other students were dropped right there) as he handed out my test papers with a large "98" marked at the top of it with a black felt marker. By golly, I was pretty darned surprised myself. Then, we ran the various combat courses in timed competition and did a lot of calisthenics with and without our rifles. Once again, I passed with flying colors or was first in the competition while others were being dropped from DI School. Like they say in beautiful down-home Kansas: "It ain't bragging if you can do it."

The last third of our total grades was comprised of "Junk-On-The-Bunk" and our competence/command presence on the drill field. From the look on Gunny Snake's face, I just knew that he planned to get me canned by one or the other challenge. As Sun Tzu wrote more than 1,000 years ago in "The Art Of War," always "know your enemy." At that time, Gunny Snake was my sworn enemy even though he was a decorated combat Marine and we were both wearing the same proud uniform. Somehow, I had to get inside of his head and prepare for the worst.

Junk-On-The-Bunk is a meticulous inspection of everything that the Marine Corps has issued each Marine. Every single article of clothing and equipment must be properly marked and laid out for inspection in an extremely precise manner. There is no room for individual interpretations. For a morning Junk-On-The-Bunk inspection, many Marines will precisely lay out their gear the night before, and then sleep on the concrete floor in their skivvies to avoid screwing up this critical display. Some will even buy extra shirts, trousers, or even shoes so that he will have a complete set ready to pass inspection at any time.

Short of cash and a tightwad as well, I did neither. So I got up before reveille and skipped breakfast that morning to catch up. At 08:00, I was ready for inspection, and so was the short red-headed Marine on the direct other side of the aisle, except that he had not yet put on his uniform. He told me that he wanted to wait until the last minute so that his uniform would be even fresher and have sharper military creases than anyone else in that Quonset hut. He was very confident with his decision and chided me for not following his example. I was not tempted. Somehow, that plan didn't sound too bright to me.

Our DI Class 19 was billeted in three Quonset huts in a row. Since the inspection party originated in the DI school headquarters to the north, the inspection team was scheduled to start in Quonset Number 1, then move south to Quonset Number 2, and finish with us on the end in Quonset Number 3. When we received the signal that the inspection team was in the first Quonset, I passed the word to Red, who said that he was going to wait until they were in the second Quonset so that he would have about 40 minutes to go.

However, the best-laid plans of redheaded corporal are often led astray, because the inspection party leapfrogged the second Quonset for some unknown reason and came directly into our Quonset. We were called to attention and the inspection began at the line of bunks on my side of the Quonset.

Junk-On-The-Bunk is always an extremely precise, demanding inspection, but in DI School it was so intense that the inspection party was absolutely focused on the items to be inspected on the bunk in front of them, and seemed unaware of everything else. Finally they arrived at my bunk, and although I could see Gunny Snake looking for something/anything to gig me, it just was not there for him so he grudgingly backed off as an imaginary black cloud seemed to envelop his head.

Finally finished with me, the inspection party did an about face, and there stood Cpl. Red at rigid attention in nothing but his green skivvies and sox. Through tight jaws, the Captain said something quietly to MSgt. Ramsey, the inspection party moved to the second bunk on that side of the Quonset and did not bother to inspect Red's bunk. He was toast. With less than a week to go before graduation, after satisfying every other physical and mental requirement while many others had fallen along the way, Red returned to his original unit and we never saw him again.

Later that evening when MSgt. Ramsey and I were sitting in his office talking about that inspection, Ramsey could only stare at his spit-shined shoes and shake his head in amused but silent wonder. In all of his 28 years in the Marine Corps (he joined in 1925), he said that he had never seen anything like that short, red-headed guy standing at ramrod attention in his green skivvies and sox beside a perfectly arranged display of all of his issued gear.

I think that Ramsey really hated to see the little guy go after he had advanced that far in such intense competition, but there was not any wiggle room to grant an exception. But maybe in the long run, that short, tough little redheaded guy may have benefitted from the experience.

Like I mentioned before, "good judgment comes from experience, and a lot of experience comes from bad judgment."

4. EVIL GENIUS

We had a tall, blond, very good-looking married guy in our DI class who had earned a perfect score (I think it was 161 or 162 at that time) on the IQ test. He was an absolute genius, and his prospects in the Marine Corps seemed boundless. However, one afternoon the entire class (down to about 45 candidates at that time) was suddenly called to an unscheduled formation on the drill field. As we stood at parade rest awaiting our turn to be inspected, an extremely pregnant young woman, two Los Angeles police officers and several Marine MPs closely inspected each man in our formation. Finally, the woman stopped in front of the handsome genius, there was a burst of unintelligible squawks back and forth, and our genius was immediately arrested and taken away in hand cuffs.

We later learned that he was the infamous serial rapist who had attacked at least one pregnant woman almost every weekend in Los Angeles for several months. That just goes to show you that you should never judge a book by its cover.

5. FORM FOR SHELTER HALVES

As I said before, all Marines take a 30-inch step at 90 steps per minute when marching in formation to get from point "A" to point "B." No more, no less, no latitude. The stride and steps per minute are exact. There is no room for deviation. "One heel, one heel" the DI chants as up to 75 boot heels hit the ground simultaneously as one. If you have ever heard that sound, you will never forget it. The well-trained, highly experienced DI turns the cadence and commands into something like a gruff song so that the cadence is always precisely the same, even many years later. However, most music majors need not apply.

The most difficult, arcane formation on any parade ground was "Form For Shelter Halves" which had something like two dozen individual commands to open the platoon side to side, then front to rear as I remember, but don't hold me to the 24 commands after more than 60 years. The M1 rifles were stacked upright in groups of three, the field marching packs were removed, the canvas-like shelter halves (each was one half of a pup tent) were removed, the tents on their folded poles were erected, the tent pegs were not driven in the ground except on dirt drill fields, and then each two Marines stood at parade rest at each side of the open flap end of the laid-out pup tent.

Each command was sharp and clear, and the final formation had to be precisely aligned from front-to-rear and side-to-side. Except for a few Old Corps DI's (from the "wooden ships and iron men" era), to my knowledge no one after WWII ever performed that maneuver except maybe for beer bets in enlisted men's slop chutes (i.e., beer bars). In fact, most Marines in 1953 had never heard that series of commands. And don't bother looking for it in the current "Landing Party Manual" because it went out after Korea when Marines in the field no longer carried those shelter halves around.

Reading the tea leaves, I was absolutely sure that was the series of commands with which Gunny Sgt. Snake would ambush me on the last day and the last test in DI school. Somehow, I just knew it. So I studied it for more than three weeks; day and night whenever I had a spare minute or more. I broke it into four distinct series and extended the preparatory commands in a verbal two-count hesitation before each barked command of execution. When I finally had it down pat, I told nearly every guy in our class that Gunny Snake would try to fail me on the last day with the "Form For Shelter Halves" series of commands, so that each candidate would be sure to bring all of the prerequisite equipment in their field marching packs and be ready to perform at a rapid, uninterrupted tempo. I even had a few dry runs with the guys in my squad at the far other end of parade grounds (huge asphalt drill field) and behind the base movie theater where no instructor from the DI School was likely to see us practicing those maneuvers over and over again.

Finally, DI Class 19 of 1953 fell out on the parade grounds (sometimes called the "grinder") where Gunny Snake called each DI candidate front and center, and announced the random marching maneuver to be performed. Since we had an unusually large class for this last stage of training, most candidates had very abbreviated appearances; something like: "Atten..hutt. Left...face. Forward... march. To the rear...march. To the rear...march. Platoon...halt. Right...face. Parade...rest." And then another candidate would be called front and center, and we would go through another brief routine.

That rain dance went on for well over an hour. Although I was the Squad Leader for the First Squad, I was not called front and center until the last man to qualify. With a dead-pan lack of expression, Gunny Snake announced my qualifying drill field maneuver: "Form For Shelter Halves."

"Aye aye, Sir. Atten...hutt. Dress right...dress." Then I took that whole platoon through the entire maneuver in cadence, and by the numbers as smooth as a black cat's fanny. Then I reversed the order and put them back into a platoon formation by the numbers in a little over a minute while Gunny Snake's mouth actually fell open as he watched in utter amazement as every man in the platoon bit his tongue or inner cheek and tried very hard not to laugh out loud. As I returned platoon command to Gunny Snake, over his sagging shoulder and about 50 yards beyond, I could see MSgt. Ramsey standing in the shade of the Administration Building as he watched the whole performance...with approval?

The next day when I received my orders right after our graduation ceremony and class photograph (figure 8), I was one of only three newly minted DIs who were immediately assigned to various recruit platoons as working DIs. All of the remainder of the graduates were assigned to a DI pool on the base, or were sent to Camp Mathews as rifle coaches.

Thank you, Sun Tzu, you murderous old Mongolian motivator, you. I read your book.

Figure 8. Drill Instructors School, Class 19 Graduation

6. FROM OCS TO FLIGHT TRAINING

Bad News. When I graduated from boot camp, our scheduled OCS training at Quantico was suddenly set back from August 1953 to February 1954. That was no big deal for me because I was still getting sorted out as a Marine, and I knew that I needed a lot more time to get my sea legs. But then, while I was in DI School, my OCS starting date was pushed back again, this time to July 1954. Apparently, Quantico's dance card was full to overflowing with a gaggle of new college graduates who yearned to look good in Marine officer "dress blues, spit-shined shoes and a light coat of oil."

About that time, I began to wonder if I should get on over to Korea and take care of my original reason for joining. Shooting left handed, left eyed, I was confident that I could darned well score Sharpshooter and maybe even Expert on a standard day with no weather problems to deal with. That was my story and I stuck with it. If a Marine sniper would be a casualty, I would be comfortable picking up his special rifle and using it to even the score with the Korean and ChiCom Bad Guys.

But then, after I had been a working DI with a recruit platoon, the word came down that a dozen enlisted men out of the 194,000 active duty enlisted Marines in the Corps were going to be sent to Pensacola, Florida for flight training. The big, mind-boggling surprise: I was one of that 12. Say what? I could not believe it, so I double checked with the MCRD Personnel pogues before I could accept any part of that narrative. What irony! I sure as heck had not applied for Flight School, and with my known head and other injuries some years before and that little red/green color diffugalty on the side, I was nevertheless one of the small group of enlisted Marines chosen for flight training. That was a horse of a different color. Hopefully, it was not a dull red or dull green. Those were not my favorite colors, and I thought that the corpsmen knew it.

When I joined the Marines as enlisted cannon fodder for Korea, a finely tuned color sense did not matter worth a flip. I was an available warm body, and I could shoot running rabbits and other small game as well as anybody and better than most, and live in a "lean-to" canvas shelter outside quite comfortably long before I went to tent camp at the rifle range at Camp Mathews.

But then, when I just barely failed the color test for OCS after having passed it once before, I was sent to the Navy Hospital at Balboa one afternoon and took a color test with dazzling bright fuzzy strings like Screaming Yellow Zonkers, Outburst Orange and Dazzling Sunburst Red. I was able to pick out all but the green string, so I saved it and the brown string until the last, and then I aced the green string by elimination after I picked the brown string, which left only one string still to identify, and only one color that had not been picked. Shazam! I broke the code with the last piece in the puzzle and won another round with those nasty eyeball purists; bless their evil, little black hearts.

Despite my injuries before joining the Marines to get even with the North Koreans and their Chinese communist allies, I really believed that I was as good a Marine as any, and possibly a wee bit better than others. Since I always recovered fully and rapidly, naturally I put all of those injuries behind me and basically forgot about them for the most part.

For example, during my senior year at St. Mary's High School in Wichita, I was clipped from behind while rushing the passer as a defensive end—a "No No" that earned our opponents a 10-yard penalty—by a very large, no neck, mouth-breathing fullback who broke my leg just above my ankle. Four weeks later, I was back on the gridiron starting at left offensive and defensive tackle, essentially paired off to block Pug Prather, who was the biggest, baddest, toughest defensive lineman on the state champion Wichita North High School football team in 1950. Much bigger than me, Pug did not get many tackles that night, and no sacks at all. Our football coach, Carmen "Rip" DePascal, was still talking about that David-and-Pug Goliath matchup at our class's 50th reunion in 2001.

When I had that cerebral hemorrhage in mid-November of 1950, complete with amnesia and aphasia, I was out of the hospital just before Christmas, back in school by mid-February of 1951, relearned a metric potful of words and names, took tests to makeup all of the class work that I had missed, and then lettered in varsity baseball with a high batting average by that April although batting helmets were yet to be invented. I really liked to play baseball.

That summer, after all of those supposedly debilitating injuries, I played semi-professional baseball for the Roscum Realtors team in the National Semi-pro Championship Tournament, and received my first of two contract offers from the Boston Red Sox farm system. That fall, I played first-string varsity offensive and defensive end on a football scholarship from El Dorado Junior College: now Butler County Community College. On kickoffs and punts, I was on the field whether we kicked or received, so I pretty much believed that I had fully recovered and could forget about it. Wouldn't you?

Then there was that mental acuity thing. After my concussions and cerebral hemorrhages, I made some fairly good scores on my IQ tests, so naturally I did not believe those injuries were much of an accumulative problem either.

Knowing that I was blessed to recover quickly from all kinds of injuries, quite naturally I really, truly believed that I had fully recovered from my cerebral hemorrhages just the way that I knew that

I had recovered from broken bones, concussions, a falling brick that removed three of my teeth at a construction job, and all of those other inconvenient injuries.

7. WHAT GOES AROUND COMES AROUND.

I remembered when Pfc. "Groaner" (not his real name) was just back from more than a year in Korea and had applied to attend DI School. However, the billets were all full at that time so he had to wait at the rifle range for an opening to DI School. When my recruit Platoon 118 arrived at Camp Mathews at least one DI short to accommodate that tent-camp syllabus, Pfc. Groaner got his chance to temporarily act as a backup DI although he was not qualified at that time.

Unfortunately, Pfc. Groaner was a sadist who enjoyed putting a hurting on an entire platoon of recruits just because he could. Overworked, our other DIs apparently did not notice, or they were just too darned busy in tent camp to give two hoots in Hades. So Pfc. Groaner amused himself by having us do various simple calisthenics like the "up and on shoulders" exercise with our M1 rifles, laying on our backs and lifting our legs at 90 steps each minute as if marching, and other simple things like that.

These were basic exercises when each was done in moderation. However, this sadistic meathead insisted that we do them for something ridiculous like 10 minutes or more on each exercise until the pain had every one in our recruit platoon straining way beyond any reasonable level until finally many fell out hurting and exhausted. There was no excuse for that kind of maltreatment except that Groaner just loved to put a lot of pain on the entire platoon when he finally got the chances.

Then, wonder of wonders, months later when I was just about to graduate from DI School, Groaner finally got his billet and arrived at the school in advance of his then-forming class of 60 or more candidates. I could not believe such good fortune when I ran into him in the head (i.e., toilet) Quonset hut, where I casually asked him a leading question: i.e., since I had taken three weeks of him, could he take three minutes of me? He guessed wrong.

Almost every Marine recruit prays for that opportunity during boot camp, and I did not waste the opportunity. Pfc. Groaner started his DI training with a much improved if badly bruised attitude, among other battered and bruised body parts. One thing I know for sure, there is a God in Heaven, and He really cares about His Marine recruits.

8. U.S. MARINE QUOTE

"Why in hell can't the Army do it if the Marines can? They are the same kind of men; why can't they be like Marines?"

General John J. "Black Jack" Pershing, Commanding General, U.S. Army in France, 12 February 1918.

IV. JUNIOR DRILL INSTRUCTOR WITH PLATOON 205

1. RECRUIT MALTREATMENT

Three senior DIs and I picked-up Recruit Platoon 205 at the receiving barracks, and soon had their heads shaved, uniforms and 782 web gear issued, and all of the other preparatory stuff like that. On the second or third day, we marched them to the outdoor boxing ring behind the base theatre where a highly respected Marine major, who had been awarded the Congressional Medal of Honor, gave them their boot camp orientation lecture. About halfway through his talk, the major startled me by announcing: "And now, I will tell you about maltreatment."

"Good Lord," I thought as I was starkly jolted to complete attention. "Now we will have a whole darned platoon of sea lawyers." I was dreading his next sentence until he continued by saying: "Your Drill Instructor can NOT brand you." Then he changed the subject to something entirely unrelated. After that, we had one of the most responsive, respectful, hard-working platoons of former hippies and spoiled mama's boys at the Marine Corps Recruit Depot (MCRD) at San Diego, California.

2. "SIR. WHERE IS THE BEER, SIR?"

Pvt. Gunther G. was the first of many surprises. Pvt. Gunther was a former farm boy from the German-American triangle in northwestern Kansas. His dad may have been a Prussian hard nose because Pvt. Gunther was far more squared away than most raw recruits, although he had a strong Teutonic accent and did have some problems communicating with people who were not from the German triangle of northwestern Kansas. I am proud to say that with time and training, he become a fine Marine and an expert rifleman.

However, when he first approached me and asked permission to speak to me after evening chow, he was confused and seemed to be intensely concerned. His problem, he could not find the beer spigot in the chow hall. No kidding. The other recruits in the platoon had insisted that beer was not served in Marine Recruit chow halls or, for that matter, any other enlisted Marine chow halls. As I already knew from working on a wheat harvest in the Fort Hays/Schinshuen area of Kansas many years before, the German farmers drank beer with their meals, and Pvt. Gunther wanted to know where it was kept so that he could get his fair share of his favorite beverage with his meals.

The lad was quite disturbed and dead serious. So I explained to him that his fellow recruits were absolutely right. In fact, I explained it to him twice because he just could not get it through his head the first time that we did not serve beer in boot camp, but that he could buy some beer at the enlisted Marine slop chute after he graduated from boot camp.

Obviously the Marine recruiters back in Hays, Kansas had not mentioned that little discrepancy when Pvt. Gunther signed on the dotted line. Golly, if you cannot trust your local Marine recruiter, who can you trust?

That reminded me of an old adage I heard from Mr. Cowboy, the busted up old night clerk at the Royal Hotel in El Dorado, Kansas where I slept in a converted coal storage room in the basement during much of my freshman year in college. Always cheerful although sporting a really crooked smile from apparently getting kicked smack dab on his chin by a Brahma bull or a bucking bronco in his youth, Mr. Cowboy also limped kind of sideways, apparently from being stomped by the same animals back during his wild and wooly rodeo days. Anyway, Mr. Cowboy was my good friend and source of unwavering good advice. For a situation something like that above, Mr. Cowboy would tell me pearls of wisdom like: "lettin' the cat out of the bag is a whole lot easier than puttin' it back in." Mr. Cowboy was a very smart old buckaroo.

3. PVT. PARIS WAS TOUGH

As a former college football defensive end, I gained a full measure of attention and a metric potful of respect from my recruits when I picked out the two biggest recruits in the platoon (both of whom were bigger than me and had played high school football) and challenged each of them to try to block me. Both were eager to take a shot at a DI. However, each time I knocked the stuffing out of them on my early count; i.e., I started moving a microsecond before they did. Bouncing them off the barrack's wall like that really did not hurt anyone, but it certainly gave them and the whole platoon a large measure of physical respect for this left-handed junior DI.

However, there was a huge, squarish but soft-spoken Neanderthal of a kid, Pvt. Paris, who had gotten badly cut across the palm of his hand by a broken glass bottle (that's his story and he stuck with it) on his way to boot camp. Quietly determined, he would not let that slow him down one bit as a boot recruit. That young fellow was plenty tough enough to get away with it.

Every morning as the entire platoon stood at attention in their skivvies by their bunks after reveille, I would check Pvt. Paris' wounded hand under the bandage. Although it was still a bloody mess, he would always say: "Sir. The private's hand is fine. Sir!" Knowing he was not going to play any football with me that day, I then confronted the assembled recruits with: "Any of you $*&#@& people want to play football with me today?" Few ever did, and none ever won. However, if Pvt. Paris had been blessed with a miraculous recovery, I might have changed my morning spiel a bit. That recruit spoke softly, but he carried a huge load of muscle and determination. I knew that he would make a fine Marine, and I was proud to be a part of his training.

4. PVT. JERRELES LITERALLY SHINED

One of my recruits, a large, tall, hard-charging African-American guy named Pvt. Jerreles was already so efficient at spit shining shoes, cleaning uniforms/rifles and other gear that I was challenged to keep him busy all of the time as required. One guy doping off can ruin a platoon's cohesion very quickly. Finally, as a last resort, when he was finished working with his gear and every other recruit was far behind him, I had him re-shine his shoes, then the senior DI's spare shoes and then re-iron a few of our uniforms as well as his own. That worked pretty well. He seemed to enjoy the extra effort and the well-earned recognition.

Then, one day as my platoon was waiting to assemble outside the chow hall after lunch, another recruit, Pvt. Bernard Kendall (my roommate in college) approached Pvt. Jerreles and asked him if Platoon 205 had a DI named Ferman, and if so, what kind of a Marine was this Ferman guy?

Pvt. Jerreles said proudly to Pvt. Kendall: "Oh, he's shaaarp; and I makes him that way."

Like Mac Davis often sang: "Oh Lord It's Hard To Be Humble, When You Are Perfect In Every Way."

5. THEY CAN'T KEEP BILL BRILL DOWN

At the afternoon mail call in July 1953, I got a letter from my grade school, high school and college buddy, Bill Brill, who was in a Navy hospital in Japan. However, that letter was written in flowery and delicate female handwriting. The letter said that Bill had been wounded by a ChiCom 120mm mortar shell (that's the big one) that had essentially vaporized his fellow Marine next to him in the last days of the Korean War. Some Chinese grunt probably hated to waste a mortar round that he had humped all of the way from the Yalu River down to South Korea and he did not want to carry it back home.

As the result, a Navy nurse was writing the letter for Bill because he was blinded (fortunately that was temporarily). Bill said that the doctors had told him that he may never walk again. Bill concluded his letter with: "Bull shit! I'll not only walk again, but I will run again."

Several years later, Bill Brill was the first-string fullback at Kansas University. I never cease to be impressed with that tough but soft-spoken guy. The thing that shakes me is that many of his neighbors and even his friends in that tiny village of Sedgwick, Kansas, did not know that Bill had ever been a Marine, let alone a decorated, wounded warrior during the Korean War. There was a lot of that going around back home during and after the Korean War when returning Marine warriors were often reviled as "baby killers" and worse.

6. "SIR. I AM BLIND, SIR."

One morning, I was relaxing in another platoon's DI Duty Hut exchanging college football stories for Korean combat sea stories with an old salt Staff Sergeant over a fresh pot of hot coffee and a fresh box of Danishes. Far and away his best story was about a fairly raw recruit who knocked on the DI's Duty Hut door and requested permission to enter the Duty Hut. Commanded to enter, the recruit marched into the room smartly, did a precise left-face directly in front of the seated Senior DI as required and, after being given permission to speak, announced in all seriousness: "Sir. I am blind, Sir."

After a series of unproductive questions, the Senior DI got up and took a swing with his fist right in front of the recruit's nose. Startled, the recruit jumped back to duck the punch (it would not have hit him anyway), then returned to his original stance of attention where he repeated that he was still blind. This fiasco continued with the same routine for four or five times around the berry bush. The recruit kept ducking at each swing of the Senior DI's intentionally not-connecting fist until finally the recruit broke down crying because the Senior DI refused to believe that he was blind.

Eventually, that recruit was led stumbling and blubbering to sickbay for analyses and whatever appropriate treatment he might need. That DI told me that they never saw that kid again, so he was probably sent home to his mama where he belonged.

To quote Pfc., later full-bull Colonel George Newton Bailey: "Some cats got it, and some cats ain't."

7. "SIR. I JUST HAD AN EPILEPTIC FIT, SIR."

Several weeks later, a second recruit had no such luck when he attempted a variation on that theme in our platoon. I witnessed the whole rain dance up close and very personal. This recruit banged on the Duty Hut door several times, eventually received permission to enter, came to a rigid attention in front of the Senior DI's desk, and reported in all seriousness that he had just had an epileptic fit. Surprised, our Senior DI darned near snorted his coffee through his nose, and then ordered that recruit to immediately have another epileptic fit. The recruit's shouted response: "Sir. I cannot. Sir." The Senior DI jumped up from his chair, got eyeball-to-eyeball with the recruit and yelled: "You will have an epileptic fit if I tell you to have an epileptic fit. Do you hear me, boy?"

That rain dance continued back and forth for several minutes. Finally, since the recruit did have a runny nose by that time as well as a hacking cough, I was ordered to take him to the sick bay where he was thoroughly checked out that afternoon, and then he was returned to duty since no epileptic symptoms were found during his tests in the sickbay and, according to our Right Guide and squad leaders, nobody in our platoon heard or saw anything unusual like an epileptic fit. Especially in a crowd of 75 recruits in a fairly small area, no one could just miss a guy having an epileptic fit.

From that day forward, we treated that recruit just like every other recruit. However, whenever he had a fire watch or wash line watch at night by himself, the junior DI (yours truly) had to also be on duty, but out of sight while watching him in case he might actually have an epileptic fit and need immediate medical attention. I lost a lot of sleep because of that rascal, so I was darned glad when he finally settled down and turned into a darned good Marine.

8. MAMA'S BOY.

There was a sniveling, crybaby mama's boy in one of the competition platoons who should never have bragged his way into my Marine Corps in the first place. He just did not pack the gear. However, that twerp did not get the word until way too late to dance out the gate cleanly. Although he tried all kinds of silly ruses to drop out without a dishonorable discharge, he only became more and more entangled deeper and deeper into steaming kimshee, and picked up more and more punishment details for not only himself, but also his fellow recruits. That is not the way to make friends and influence the All Mighty Powers That Be in boot camp.

Finally, during qualification at the rifle ranges at Camp Mathews, mama's misguided little man somehow figured that an accidental foot wound would get him a nice, neat, medical discharge. Unfortunately, this misplaced recruit had no idea of the force of the M1 rifle's muzzle blast. When he tried to shoot himself neatly at the meaty edge of his foot so as to avoid damaging any of his useful bones, the M1 muzzle blast tore off his whole foot up to his ankle.

Like the rodeo-crippled, old, night clerk at the Royal Hotel in El Dorado, Kansas and my occasional philosophical mentor, Mr. Cowboy, once told me that "The biggest trouble maker you'll ever have to deal with; he watches you shave his face in the mirror every morning."

9. M1 THUMB: PRETTY DARNED DUMB

The M1 Girand rifle is a marvelously effective, deadly weapon that can reach out and accurately "touch" bad guys at ranges of 500 yards or more with nothing more than the iron sights. However, when preparing for M1 rifle inspection on the parade ground with the bolt slid to the rear, you press down and release the ammo-magazine feed mechanism that releases the spring-loaded bolt, which slams forward and can painfully smash the thumb of many unwary boot recruits. That fairly common faux pas is called an "M1 thumb." Since I was such a kind, caring, conscientious, left-handed, handsome DI who did not want any of my raw recruits to suffer any unauthorized pain, I carefully demonstrated to the entire platoon just how that could happen if they weren't careful.

Somehow, lost in the eloquent flow of my own lecture, I did not remove my thumb properly so there I was, standing tall in front of

75 recruits with an M1 rifle firmly and agonizingly attached to my throbbing right thumb. As "Mr. Marine Corps" to these recruits, I could not even grimace or give the slightest hint of the pain I was suffering as I finished my lecture to a now convinced and attentive platoon, many of whom were sure that I had done that stupid faux pas to myself on purpose for their edification. All of that time, my two senior DIs were standing by stoically behind the platoon watching—but not rendering any assistance—to see how the heck I would get myself out of that stupid, self-induced mess.

As my Irish relatives occasionally say: "Anything can happen, and always does."

10. RECRUITS SNORE BY THE NUMBERS

Since so many activities in boot camp were performed by the numbers, we took it one step further when we put the platoon to bed by the numbers. That worked really well, but I had a hard time keeping a straight face at the beginning. With each successive night, going to bed by the numbers became the norm for Platoon 205. It went something like the following as the duty DI called out each number loud and clear:

"One."   All recruits stood at attention by their bunks in their skivvies
"Two."   The recruits pulled down their top sheets and covers
"Three." They got into their bunks and lay on their backs at attention.
"Four." They pulled up their top sheets and covers and lay at attention. Then the DI said in a conversational tone of voice: "Good night, men" and of course they replied in unison: "Sir. Good night, Sir." The DI invariably bellowed: "I can't HEAR you." The recruits bellowed back as loud as they could: "SIR. GOOD NIGHT, SIR."
"Five." The recruits would lay at rigid attention with their eyes closed while they made snoring noises.

The DI then turned off the lights in the squad bay. That whole drill may sound silly to the uninitiated, but it worked for me and the other

DIs, and substantially cut down on recruit scuttlebutt after lights out. However, after all of the recruits were settled in for the night, from a far corner of the barracks or Quonset hut, the pathetic wail of the unknown boot recruit was often heard to say: "I'M…NOT… HAPPY…HERE."

11. ALL-AMERICAN PULLING GUARD WAS DISCHARGED.

Somehow, all roads always seemed to lead back to football. Because of my undeclared head injuries (undeclared because nobody asked), I preferred to be just a punter, as well as point-after-touchdown (PAT) and field goal kicker for the MCRD football team. From my college clippings and a grand demonstration of kicking for hang time and distance, I had that job pretty much locked up at that time. However, the MCRD football coach also wanted me to play offensive and/or defensive end. That was a bit worrisome because MCRD had a four-year college-level football team that played other four-year college-level football teams. These guys were very big and darned tough, so playing on the line could possibly rattle my pots and pans or reinjure my hands before I could get even when Korea would eventually boil over again. After all, that was the reason why I joined the Marines.

However, suddenly the team's overall potential took a huge leap forward when one of the All-American pulling guards joined the Marines after completing his four years of eligibility at a major university. In my mind's eye, I could just see me blocking a defensive tackle, end or linebacker as our new All-American guard would lead the interference on a whole bunch of power sweeps around my left end. Together, I figured that we would rip humungous holes in anybody's defenses, and I would also get to kick a heck of a lot of PATs while the best looking BAMs (women Marines) assembled from all over southern California would swing their pom poms and other good stuff with gay abandon.

I guarantee you that I was fully torqued and ready to go for it. I figured that taking that chance could be worth the gamble. I could not wait for football season to begin. Recruit Platoon 205, Charley

Company would have to find a new junior DI on whom to dump most of the hard stuff.

Two weeks later, everything turned to clabber. Our new All-American superstar was discharged from my Marine Corps. Why? Why? Why? Even in a slow-learners' "900 platoon" that had an 18-week boot camp instead of 12 weeks, our All-American guard was not trainable. This guy, who had been academically eligible for football for four years at that major university nearby, could not pass a written test or much else academically. I know for sure that my Marine Corps gave him every chance possible to stay in the Corps because we wanted him to help raise our game to a higher level

Besides that, the base commanding general really wanted a winning football team, and the rest of the MCRD football team sure as heck wanted him to stick around and do his thing as well. However, when all was said and done, a whole bunch of "littles" made an unacceptable "much" and our All-American pulling guard was discharged from my Marine Corps.

I've got to admit that USMC recruits did not need to be magna cum loudly to be good mud Marine Grunts, and that goes double for any All-American pulling guards, especially just a few months before the fall football season was about to begin. But when all was said and done, no matter how we could slice it, there was no way on God's green earth that we could keep that hard-charging, incomparable football star either in our lineup or in Marine green.

Like my dear old Mom often said back when I was a little kid and would get the Big Eye for some dime toy in the Sears toy department: "Wantin' ain't gettin'."

12. "HUTT, TWO, THREE, FIVE" (?)

Although I gave him my best shot, I really struck out with Pvt. (I'll call him Tucker), who was a pretty smart kid, but apparently had always walked with an exaggerated long, kind of bowlegged stride like Lil' Abner over a plowed field in the comic strip of the same name. Therefore, he was always out of step with the platoon within three steps or less. Being the junior DI in Platoon 205, the Senior DI assigned me to take Pvt. Tucker aside from the platoon and give him one-on-one private instructions to get him sorted out until he would be able to march with the rest of the platoon.

For the better part of a week, I marched Pvt. Tucker all by himself as I chanted cadence so that he could learn mentally as well as physically to keep in step with my regulation 30-inch pace at exactly 90 steps each minute. Long story short, he and I did all of the basic parade ground drill maneuvers over and over again in cadence, by the numbers while marching side-by-side.

We essentially followed the platoon wherever it went. But each time that I thought I had him trained, as soon as he returned to the platoon, he reverted to that darned Lil' Abner stride and fouled up the rest of the platoon unless, of course, he was the last guy in the squad formation. But then, after the first "To the rear...march" command, he would be leading his squad and screwing up everybody in the platoon again.

I hate to admit it, but I was mui thankful when Pvt. Tucker caught the flu and had to be set back a week or so with another platoon to frustrate another junior DI. I had taken my best shot and had nothing to show for all of that effort. I think I know what you are thinking. Like that old country/western song says: "Here's A Quarter, Call Someone Who Cares."

13. POINTY RECRUIT BAYONETS

While we were at the rifle range at Camp Mathews, one of our recruits (I'll call him Pvt. White for privacy reasons) was seen sharpening his bayonet with a whet stone. That was an absolute "No No;" forbidden throughout boot camp although the point stays wickedly sharp, and every Marine sharpened his bayonet during the boat ride to Korea. As a temporary, on-loan, junior DI and rifle coach (I'll call him Cpl. Lee because I can't remember his name after all of these years), checked it out, Pvt. White suddenly jumped up from his rack with a crazy wild-eyed expression on his face and the sharpened bayonet in his hand as he tried to skewer Cpl. Lee "long, wide, deep, frequent and continuously."

Not too big, but fast on his feet, Cpl. Lee ran by our DI Duty Tent leading Pvt. White and yelling about what was happening, and what he was going to do as Pvt. White screamed gibberish and stabbed the air wildly just a few feet behind him. As more DIs came running from nearby platoons, Cpl. Lee led Pvt. White in a big circle through the rows of tents and then led him back down the same path where a mob of DIs jumped on Pvt. White, pretty much clobbered him until he turned loose of the bayonet, then hustled him off to the base MPs, who immediately took him to the camp sick bay where he obviously belonged.

We never saw Pvt. White again and that was okay with everybody. When dealing with live ammo, bayonets, and other things that go kaboom every day, there is no room for basket cases with certifiably bad attitudes.

As luck would have it, I watched that whole rain dance from afar because I was in the hand grenade pits working on my technique since I had never thrown a live grenade in combat. Most of the other DIs had already passed that test in Korea or during WWII in the Pacific Theatre of that war. However, a few of those guys still did not have the arm to accurately throw a grenade for demonstration purposes, so I was told to be ready if needed. Before I could teach our recruit platoon, I needed to be very good at throwing that tricky but doubly deadly weapon.

Like they say, "close" only counts with horse shoes and hand grenades. Well doggone it, I am here to tell you that "close" counts a heck of a lot more with a hand grenade than it counts with any darn horse shoe. You can take that to the bank.

14. NOT LIKE JOHN WAYNE

Like I said before, I was getting ready to help introduce our recruits to a practice hand grenade that looked and weighed exactly the same as the real thing, but was not configured with a full charge or deadly shrapnel. However, that small training aid was fairly darned dangerous anyway because it could blow away a finger or two, or possibly blind somebody in the blink of an eye. Bottom line, there was the wrong way to throw that grenade (like John Wayne's soft hook shots in several popular but inaccurate movies), and then there was the Marine way which was, of course, the right way.

I had opted for an intense refresher by the numbers and a lot of practice before I was anywhere near confident enough to help train a platoon of recruits whose lives could depend upon this training in only a few months. Fortunately, Sgt. Somebody, I'll call him Ed (remember, this was 65 years ago), was a veteran of both intense house-to-house battles for Seoul, Korea right after the 1st Marine Division's game-changing landing at Inchon. Since hand grenades were often the weapon of choice in those battles, Sgt. Ed got the rose and I backed him up.

During the recruit training session, Sgt. Ed was in the practice pit with the recruit who had fired expert the day before, our senior DI stood back from the pit grading each recruit as well as Sgt. Ed and the junior DI (me) from next to a wall of sand bags. The other DIs and rifle coaches were with the rest of the platoon watching at a safe distance. Despite clear, straightforward instructions, the first recruit threw the first grenade very poorly with something more like the standard John Wayne-type overhead, lazy hook-shot delivery that is hardly ever accurate, especially beyond a dozen yards or so.

It was surprising how hard it was to overcome inherent bad habits with young recruits who grew up playing war games and watching John Wayne movies where ol' John would say something laconic about a pilgrim or a bad guy, pull that heavy duty cotter pin with his teeth (say what?), then toss that soft hook shot for a perfect bull's eye on the bad guys every single time. Good luck if you try that stupid trick when your life is on the line. The recruit's grenade exploded nowhere near the target.

So Sgt. Ed showed the next recruit in even more detail how to throw a grenade from his ear somewhat like a football with a follow-through more like a baseball catcher tossing a baseball back to the pitcher. Apparently scared out of his gourd from having a live practice grenade in his hand that could actually hurt him more than somewhat, that obviously shook-up recruit was initially hesitant, finally pulled the cotter pin with some difficulty (surprise, surprise, it's a fairly burly cotter key that could chip or break even John Wayne's pearly white teeth), and in the process he choked up, the now-armed training grenade slipped backwards out of his shaky, sweaty fingers as his arm moved backwards, and the grenade landed at their feet in the training pit armed and ready to reach out and touch both of those guys.

The senior DI yelled: "Stuff it in the hole," and everybody above ground disappeared behind the sandbags. In what seemed like adrenaline-induced slow motion, Sgt. Ed calmly shoved the loose grenade into the post hole and then grabbed the recruit and dived to the other end of the fighting hole. The practice grenade exploded, but the blast could not hurt anyone from deep in the dirt at the bottom of the safety post hole. However, the recruit tossed his cookies all over his boondocker boots, and even shared some barf on Sgt. Ed's boondockers as well.

After everyone was sorted out and their boondockers cleaned off, Sgt. Ed asked me if I wanted to instruct the next and last recruit. As I looked at the sweaty, four-eyed kid with 10 thumbs coming forward for his reluctant turn, I held my arms straight out in front of me with both hands pointed vertically and my fingers spread wide apart, stepped back a few steps, and told Sgt. Ed that I thought that he was doing just fine so there was no need to switch places.

My mom didn't raise any fools.

15. PROFANE BAM DI

Back at MCRD, as a working DI with the white duty belt and occasionally the platoon leader's symbolic saber to prove it, I was privileged to take a shortcut from our platoon's Quonset huts directly to the PX on a straight line by passing through the Woman Marine (BAM) recruit training area. That entire complex was off-limits to all other-than-DI male Marines on the base, although it cut quite a bit off the walk to get from the south side to the north side of the base where the Post Exchange (PX) and the slop chutes (enlisted beer bars) were located.

One morning as I walked through that shortcut past a 75 BAM recruit platoon that was facing me at parade rest while their BAM DI had her back toward me and may not have known that I was passing through No Man's Land. As I passed close behind her due to a choke point formed by two buildings, the potty mouthed BAM DI let loose a burst of profanity the likes of which few male recruits would ever be exposed. No kidding. I was so surprised and mortified by her graphic descriptions of private female and male body parts (the use and abuse thereof) that I hesitated for a moment to absorb the full brunt of that woman's vitriol spewed on those very young women who, I would bet, had never even imagined that type of overwhelming profanity in their lives back in 1953. FYI: I never used that shortcut again.

Actually, the term BAM is a fairly common but unofficial acronym for "Big Assed Marine." However, most male Marines have used that officially forbidden acronym in their barracks and among themselves so often that it seeped out into the real world on occasion. In fact, when confronted, a young Marine 2nd lieutenant avoided a backlash from a superior officer by swearing that he always thought that "BAM" stood for "Beautiful American Marine."

Nice try, shave tail, Sir. I had to bite my lip to keep from snorting out loud and blowing his whole silly story to pieces.

16. THE REVEREND RECRUIT

One of our recruits was a youngish, kind of baby faced Methodist minister. I kid you not. That was bad news, but even worse news was that this Methodist minister knew the Senior DI's dad, who was also a Methodist minister. Why he was not commissioned as a Navy chaplain I will never know. Maybe it was another of those strange experiments that come along every once in a while. But needless to say, having an ordained minister as a recruit in our platoon inhibited the heck out of the traditional Marine DI way of encouraging our recruits and getting things done efficiently in the proven Marine way.

Finally, with a lot of almost pleading encouragement from the Senior DI, I took the Pvt/minister recruit aside and explained to him that we just could not treat him special in any way or change our distinct DI vocabulary as that would not produce the type of Marine needed to win wars. Fortunately, he readily understood and agreed to that logic pretty much, so we all went back to our old tried-and-true DI ways, and that subject was never mentioned again.

Long story short, the minister/recruit graduated as an excellent Marine Pfc. I hope that he later applied for a commission as a Navy chaplain, and the boot camp experience did him a world of good when he would become a commissioned chaplain. At least, I will bet that he was a far better shooter with the M1 rifle and the M1911 Colt semi-automatic pistol than your average Methodist minister.

God does indeed move in mysterious ways.

17. FATHER O'BRIAN'S BOMB BAY

Navy Commander/Reverend Father O'Brian, over whose office door hung the sign: "O'Brian's Bomb Bay – Come In And Get Blasted" was a combat-veteran chaplain and good friend who enjoyed hitting me pretty hard on my shoulder almost every time that we met, even if I had 75 recruits under my direct command at that moment.

One day, he and I were talking off the record in his office and Father O'Brian mentioned that he knew that there were places on MCRD where he could find recruit maltreatment at almost any time of day or night. But he added that he would not press the issue because he knew from his terrible experiences at the "Frozen Chosin Reservoir" battles in Korea that to survive on the battlefield, these young Marines had to learn to be tough, resilient and resourceful; exactly the way we trained them to be.

Fr. O'Brian was convinced that Marine boot camp, with all of its warts and blemishes, was the main reason that Marines could fight and win for month after month against such extreme odds and in such an awfully uninhabitable place as the snow-covered mountains in war-torn North Korea in the worst of the winter season. We were in total agreement, but he continued to punch my shoulder as a greeting every time that we met. However, each time that he smacked me on my shoulder with his fist, I responded in a straight-faced, detached military manner and asked in a loud parade-ground voice for everyone to hear: "Did that hurt your hand, Sir?"

That worked for me, and Father O'Brian seemed to get a kick out of it as well.

18. "BUT WHEN THE CHAPLAIN GOES HOME…"

Remembering Fr. O'Brian reminds me of a couple of often used DI spiels which were always delivered after a recruit made a gross mistake and with the DI's nose about two inches from the errant recruit's nose in the loudest parade ground voice that I could muster. That's pretty darned loud. My recruits could identify my voice from all other DI's voices on the multiple-use blacktop "grinder" from clear across the parade ground, which is about 90 yards wide and several hundred yards long. The trick is to speak from the diaphragm and not just with your vocal cords. Try it, you will like it.

The first spiel was always given to the entire platoon during a particularly difficult event. When necessary, I would bellow: "I am your drill instructor, your brother in arms, your Uncle Sam. And when the chaplain goes home, I…AM… GOD… ALL…MIGHTY!" Of course, that was just a figure of speech meaning that I was the final authority as far as they were concerned. However, some of our recruits, under all of the sometimes extreme stress normal to Marine boot camp, seemed to momentarily believe that like Zeus, I could call down thunder and lightning and other bad stuff on demand. Actually, there were times that I would have if I could have.

The second was just as loud, but always on a more personal one-on-one, nose-to-nose occasion when a recruit had really screwed up more than once. This spiel always started on a fairly even toned, conversational level and quickly built by successive increments up to my loudest parade ground voice. I always began with a personal question on a conversational level but essentially nose to nose. "Do you like me, boy?" (Then in a louder voice) "You had better not like me…BOY" (followed by a much louder voice) "…because likin' leads to lovin'" (even louder voice), "…and lovin' leads to…" Okay, forget that one and just use your imagination. That's maybe a bit too much for these civilian-directed sea stories, especially in mixed company.

One of my favorite spiels, delivered stony faced and with no show of emotion after a recruit had received a "dear john" letter from his former best girlfriend, was: "If my Marine Corps wanted you to have a girlfriend, then my Marine Corps would have issued you a girlfriend. Get over it, we've got work to do."

Funny thing though; when those first two, as well as similar routines were first used in disciplinary, get-their-attention situations, they were basic stony faced, tight-jawed, snorting and snarling theatrics. But after a couple of weeks of training 24/7 around the clock, each became even more intense and a highly emotional moment for both the DI and the recruits.

Boot camp is serious business. We make Marines. Marines win wars.

19. WORLD WAR II MOVIES

By the time that I was privileged to assist the same bayonet-training instructor who had trained platoon 118 when I was in boot camp, I had worked long and hard on my bayonet techniques, and was fairly comfortable with that quintessential Marine close-combat weapon. I believed that in the same situation in Korea, I would win one way or the other. Thank goodness I didn't have to prove that statement.

Somehow, the British had taken a fairly decent movie of actual bayonet fights during one of their many night raids across the English Channel in France before D-Day during World War II. That film brought several more training concepts home to me, and affected my basic outlook about bayonet fighting.

On that incredibly clear film due to the raging fires burning brightly in the area, we watched British commandoes racing ashore to blow up something vital when a single German soldier stood tall and took out four of those commandoes with his bayonet before he was killed. The German's bayonet techniques were outstanding. As each commando came at him with bayonet elbow-locked forward as the Brits were inclined to do, this very large German parried their bayonet thrusts aside, sliced obliquely down his enemy's neck bungee with his bayonet, smashed his opponent's chest with a vertical rifle butt stroke, bayonet his opponent in the chest or gut, then withdraw his bayonet and set himself up for his next engagement in quick succession.

That one German soldier had cleanly taken out four raiders in succession when his bayonet became stuck in his last victim's chest, who sagged to the ground as he grabbed and pulled the German's rifle and bayonet down with him, thereby leaving the German vulnerable to a fifth raider who killed the German with an unopposed bayonet thrust as the German unsuccessfully tried to jerk his bayonet out of his fourth victim's body.

After that first bayonet training session with Platoon 205, on the side I advised my recruits to try to keep a round or two in their rifles, if possible (each Marine counts each M1 shot in combat and also listens for the ping after the eighth and final round in the magazine is fired), so that if he should ever get into the same predicament as that outstanding German soldier, he will be able to pull his trigger and blow that enemy's body off the blade of his bayonet. The M1 rifle's muzzle blast is that powerful. Remember the recruit who blew his own foot off by mistake.

Although not official Marine doctrine, these were my Marine recruits and I wanted them to come home to their families after their war would be over. Besides that, any one of them could get paired off with the Chinese national bayonet champion in a kill-or-be-killed situation. In that case, when that ChiCom would set himself, I told them to shoot the bastard up close and personal, and then look around for someone else to skewer. War is not fair, and war is often fatal. I wanted my Marine warriors to come home to their families and friends in good condition, so I spent every available opportunity to hone their skills to perfection.

As stated in the Drill Instructors Creed: "These recruits are entrusted to my care. I will train them to the best of my ability. I will develop them into smartly disciplined, physically fit, basically trained Marines, thoroughly indoctrinated in love of the Corps and Country. I will demand of them and demonstrate by my own personal example, the highest standards of personal conduct, morality and professional skill." I took that creed very seriously. My Marine recruits knew that when this DI or any marine DI said that the berries are ripe, they had better go get their buckets.

By the way, my recruits did know how to "Form For Shelter Halves."

20. WEDDED BLISS: NOT IN MY BOOT CAMP.

One fine day shortly before graduation from boot camp, a recruit knocked on the duty hut door, entered, and stood at rigid attention in front of the Senior DI's desk. Respectfully, the recruit requested permission to speak to the Senior DI and, eventually he did receive permission to speak.

This fairly seasoned recruit wanted permission to marry his high school sweetheart either during or right after his boot camp graduation ceremony. His logic: wouldn't that be great to have his boot camp buddies and his whole family from back home gathered around him and his new wife on that stellar occasion?

The Senior DI almost snorted his coffee through his nose. He had never heard that particular self-centered aberration, and needed a few seconds to recover his composure. Then, in all tight-jawed seriousness, he told that recruit in no uncertain terms, once again, that if the U.S. Marine Corps had wanted the recruit to have a wife, the U.S. Marine Corps would have issued him a wife.

Then the Senior DI got up from his desk "with his hair on fire," and physically threw the bewildered recruit out of the duty hut while I held the door open and tried very hard not to snort my coffee through my nose as well.

Even in the U.S. Marine Corps, there is too-often that one percent who believe that, somehow, the world revolves around himself. I kid you not. If I could have, I would have sent that self-centered clown back through boot camp again. Maybe, he would get it right the second time around.

21. SGT. ARLEY DALE WRIGHT

Sgt. Arley Dale Wright was a fine Marine and a good friend since the summer of 1944 when we both played on the same Little League baseball team in the Wichita 10- and 11-year-old league. I played first base and Dale played second base on the T-Men team sponsored by the local employees of the U.S. Treasury Department. Two years later, we played and won what we understood was the first Little League interstate championship game after WW II when we played the

Colorado 12- to-13-year-old Little League champions, the Denver Ford baseball team at Elitch's Gardens in Denver.

Two guys on that team went on to play major league baseball: Fritzy Brickell (the son of George "Freddy" Brickell who played eight years with the Pirates and then the Phillies) initially played shortstop with the Yankees, and then I believe that he was traded to the L.A. Angels while I was catching up academically at Wichita U; and Duane Wilson, our left-handed starting pitcher who played for the Boston Red Sox. I had turned down my chance at the "Bigs" when C. B. Masterson, a scout for the Red Sox, offered me minor league contracts in both 1951 and 1952.

However, I had to turn both down because I could not afford to lose my amateur standing, and with it my football scholarship at Kansas State University, which would pay most of my legitimate bills in college. If you recall, that was the reason why Jim Thorp had to forfeit all of his Olympic medals back in the 1930s. Jim had been paid very little for playing in just a few baseball games, but any at all was too much back then.

As I kinda' sorta' mentioned before, I had played semi-pro baseball for the Roscum Realtors during the summers of 1951 and 1952, and the National Semi-Pro Championship tournaments in Wichita in one or both years. I'm positive about 1951. Everyone else on that team was paid pretty decent money for each game, and a bit more for the game that we won in the championship tournament before being eliminated by the team that I believe was the eventual champions that year. However, since even a paltry dime payment would ruin my amateur status back then, I had to take my pay after each game in six-packs and cases of beer, and charge it up to experience. Those were, indeed, the "Happy Days."

Where was I? Oh yeah, my good buddy Dale Wright. When Dale graduated from Wichita East High School, he immediately joined the Marines and became an 0311 combat infantryman, as well as a big rig truck driver. That may have sounded like easy, pleasant duty until Dale got to Korea about the same time as those humongous hordes of Chinese Communists came sneaking over the Yalu River at the frozen Chosin reservoir in the middle of a blinding blizzard. That was lousy timing because very soon the Chinese were swarming over the north side of the 38th parallel, and the Marines were dug in on the south side of the 38th parallel with orders to hold their positions, but to clobber as many Chinese as possible while the politicians on both sides of the table argued about the shape of the darn negotiating table. No kidding, you just cannot make up that kind of political crap.

Long story short, Dale's group of Marine gear heads were assigned to drive truckloads of ammunition, chow, spare parts, poopy paper, and any other essential supplies several miles up an exposed road from the supply bases in the rear with the gear to the Marine Main Line of Resistance (MLR). Under those conditions, it wasn't very long until the ChiComs had zeroed in their very accurate Russian 152-milimeter artillery on the entire exposed length of that road. That is, they had the artillery aiming data and the equipment to accurately shoot at any place on that road that their artillery spotters could see, and with time, they got pretty darned good at hitting stationary and mobile targets by timing the distance from a fixed point to another established point by the time their artillery shells took to fly to the designated impact point somewhat like leading a high flying duck with a shotgun.

So once or twice each day, Dale and his fellow truck drivers would sit in their fully loaded trucks within a narrow, safe valley until they would work up the mojo to pop their clutches, stick their right feet into their carburetors, and run that long gauntlet of artillery fire like bats out of hell. Dale arrived in Korea as a Pfc., and came back to the real world as a buck sergeant because most of the corporals and buck sergeants above him in the chain of command were eventually casualties, so he was promoted through attrition rather than time in grade.

I think that Dale was awarded the bronze star medal, but he deserved so much more than that. As I recall, Dale also got the Purple Heart when he zigged but should have zagged, but that was so long ago that I cannot remember the ribbons that he wore on his liberty uniform.

One Friday afternoon, Dale showed up at our duty hut looking for me. Later that afternoon in the base slop chute (i.e., the enlisted beer bar), Dale showed me a picture of his brand new 1953 Oldsmobile coupe that he had just bought, apparently with his accumulated combat pay. Get ready, because you probably will not believe this. Dale wanted me to drive him in his Oldsmobile to Los Angeles because he was all shook up by the traffic on U.S. Highway 5, especially over the weekend.

An astute planner, my good buddy had setup a double date for me with a "lovely young lady" in Los Angeles just to seal the deal. Unfortunately, as the Junior DI in Platoon 205, I always had the duty over the weekend. That job comes with the territory.

22. C.I.D. SPOOK IN THE RANKS

One stormy afternoon while I was cleaning muck off my boondockers in the our Duty Hut in preparation to go tromp through some more muck just for the pure joy of it, the senior DI of one of our two competition platoons visited us to pass the latest word to our senior DI. He reported that a recruit who had been in, and graduated from his DI friend's platoon about a year earlier, was now going through boot camp again with a new name. Of course, that meant that the baby faced faux recruit had to be a C.I.D. spook who was undoubtedly gathering information on either that platoon or the entire recruit training command. Holy smoke! I wondered what we were going to do to handle that situation.

In a word: we did nothing. Every DI at MCRD San Diego and rifle coach at Camp Mathews was aware of that sneaky rascal on sight. Then, the word came down from the brass on high in Charley

Company that we would change nothing. Marine Corps boot camp is intentionally physically and mentally challenging. That's the way we produce tough, knowledgeable, dedicated U.S. Marines who have mastered everything required of them (figure 9), look outstanding on the parade grounds (figure 10) and are ready to fight the enemies of the United States at any time or place and prevail.

I was very proud of that decision. Semper fi. Gung ho.

23. AMMUNITION MANAGEMENT

In combat, all mud Marine grunts are trained to communicate, maneuver, identify the enemy, get a good sight picture on that enemy, breath in and then let half of that breath out to best steady his weapon, squeeze not jerk his weapon's trigger, and always count the number of shots that he has taken so that he always knows exactly how many bullets remain in his weapon's magazine. In close combat, that can be a matter of life or going home to one's family in a box.

Figure 9. Recruit Platoon Final Inspection

Figure 10. Recruit Platoon Final Formation

An M1 rifle holds eight 30-caliber bullets/rounds in its magazine, and my favorite, the Browning Automatic Rifle (BAR), holds 20 rounds in its magazine. You do not want to see an armed enemy bad guy coming at you just when you realize that you have one less bullet than you thought you had. That is, indeed, an "Oh shit moment." Strict, disciplined, repetitive, thoughtful Marine training—based on the lessons of so many battles in so many wars—is directed to eliminate those "Oh shit moments" so that our Marines will prevail in combat and come home again to their families and friends.

Eventually, counting shots fired becomes an automatic habit that comes naturally without even thinking about it, just like old Marine 0911 (pronounced "ohh 9-11") Drill Instructors just naturally take a 30-inch stride at 90 steps per minute until too darned old (like me) or too darned hobbled (also like me) to keep up the pace. In fact, this habit takes over with regard to counting the slices of bananas I put on my morning Post Toasties, or even when I made the Sign of the Cross— touching my forehead, then my solar plexus, then my left shoulder and finally my right shoulder with my right hand while saying: "In the name of the Father, and of the Son, and of the Holy Spirit, Amen." I hate to think of all of the times that I have caught myself saying instead: "One, two, three, four." Aaarrrggg! Mea culpa.

Thank goodness that our Lord loves His U.S. Marines, so He will hopefully give us Old Corps 03-11 and 09-11 grunts an understanding pass for each such mental faux pas if we ask for it.

24. POGY BAIT MARINES

Marine recruits had no access to pogy bait during their 12 weeks of boot camp at MCRD. That meant no soda pop, no candy bars, no junk food, no tasty snacks, no anything dispensed from a vending machine and sometimes no goodies mailed from home. Marine recruits also had no choices in the chow lines either. They could eat only what was put on their metal trays in the chow line three times each day, or they could get very hungry. If a recruit doesn't like the menu, he had better pour on the Marine gravy (i.e., catsup) and choke it down or he may not have enough go-power to make it to the next meal.

I know an 85-year-old Marine who still puts catsup on his breakfast eggs (say what?), lunch and supper, and I have to admit that with time and no options whatsoever, I even learned to love "s**t on a shingle" and other infamous boot camp fare as well. However, due to a single dose of food poisoning from Mrs. Murray's sour kraut in grade school (the government dictated sour kraut that day and our old Irish school cook had never made that dish before, so her amateur brew sent every student, nun, and both priests home with the "trots"). I did not learn to choke that stuff down and it would stay down until well into the 1960s. Fortunately, the German-American recruits would trade almost anything for a second helping from my sour kraut when I was in boot camp, so the swapping lamp was always lit and I usually ate fairly well.

As I mentioned earlier, Pvt. Bernard Kendall (later SSgt B. Kendall) and I had been good buddies when we went to different high schools together in Wichita, and were roommates when we played football for the state champion El Dorado, Kansas, Junior College Grizzlies. That's why I knew how much Pvt. Kendall loved his milk shakes and cheese burgers, and how he must have been longing for a temporary change in his boot camp diet.

So one Sunday afternoon, another junior DI and I sweet talked that DI's sister into going to the Family Reception Center with us and asking to see her "half-brother," Pvt. Kendall, for an hour in the reception room. When Pvt. Kendall arrived at the center and first met his "sister" who he had never seen before, he instinctively knew enough to hug his "favorite sis" on cue, and play along until his escort returned to their platoon. Then, the other DI and his sister wandered off to swap family gossip, and Bernard was allowed to lounge on an overstuffed divan and eat cheeseburgers and chocolate milk shakes until he was good and truly stuffed while we caught up on the latest news from back home.

At the end of the allotted hour visit, I stuffed the large hand-grenade pockets in his battle jacket with enough nickel candy bars to last him quite a while, and Bernard returned to his platoon to recover from all of that luxury dining and smoozing. Naturally, I thought that I had done a really good deed for my old pal. However, years later after we had both been discharged and back at Wichita State University, I learned that his platoon buddies had offered him two dollars for each five-cent candy bar I gave him, so Bernard sold every one of that pogy bait and pocketed the loot. Somehow, the Yankee dollar had trumped Bernard's usual cravings.

After years of past experience, I was darned surprised.

25. U.S. MARINE QUOTE

When alerted by field telephone that the 1st Marine Brigade and the whole 1st Marine Division were completely surrounded by three Chinese Communist (ChiCom) Divisions during the "Frozen Chosin Reservoir" battles, iconic Marine Colonel, later Major General Lewis "Chesty" Puller, the C.O. of the 1st Marine Brigade said: "That's great. Now we can shoot in any direction. Those bastards won't get away this time."

NOTE: in that ferocious series of battles in subzero snow and ice conditions in the high mountains along the Yalu River that divides North Korea from China, the 1st Marine Division decimated all three ChiCom divisions and brought out all of their dead and wounded as well as many U.S. Army stragglers and wounded who had been abandoned by the U.S. Army as they retreated. After that mauling by our 1st Marine Division, the ChiCom high command ordered their soldiers: "Do not attack the 1st Marine Division. Leave the yellowlegs (i.e., the U.S. Marines) alone. Strike the American Army." When Colonel Chesty Puller heard about that ChiCom order to their field commanders, he ordered all of his Marines to remove their yellowish puttees so the ChiComs would have a harder time differentiating between the U.S. Marines and the U.S. Army. Colonel Chesty Puller came to Korea to fight a war and win it. He did not come to be a spectator on the sidelines. Semper fi.

V. MCRD CASUAL COMPANY

1. DEPOT LAMINATIONS

Finally, the U.S. Marine Corps made its move and pulled me out of Recruit Platoon 205 before they graduated. One minute I was up to my giblets in recruit training, and the next thing that I knew, all of us in the OCS program were pulled out from whatever each was doing and transferred to the MCRD Casual Company to await orders to either go to El Toro for more OCS mental and physical testing, or report to Camp Pendleton to get ready for the 32nd Draft to Korea.

Although the shooting war in Korea was suspended by a shaky Cease Fire Treaty at that time, the Marine Corps was more than somewhat suspicious that the North Koreans were just using that ever-stalling joehootinanny ploy to regroup, re-arm and have another go at reuniting all of Korea under one communist government. If that happened, the U.S. Marine Corps was primed and ready to finish the job that we began at the Pusan perimeter back in 1950.

Every morning after breakfast, we former DI's and rifle coaches fell out for the working parties, and every morning Pfc. D.O. Brown and I were excused from the daily working parties to report to "Depot Laminations," which sounded so important to the punchy corporal in charge of Casual Company that he never questioned our flimsy excuse day after day after day. Together, we avoided those work details like we would avoid Barney Frank's lip ice. All of us would have preferred to stay wherever we were until our final orders were cut. However, that was not to be.

To make the challenge of sneaking around in one of the most strict military bases in the world, when not catching up on our sleep in an empty dark room in the MCRD photo lab, D.O. and I would rub red Mexican bricks on rough concrete, wet the resultant powder and make red war paint which we wore on our faces all morning until we cleaned up for lunch. We were never caught although it was awfully close a couple of times. If caught, our prefab story was that like all good Marines, we were practicing our urban camouflage under the most challenging conditions imaginable. What could they do; send us to Korea? For crying in the beer, we already had one foot in that pipe line, and were ready to boogie on over to Korea any day and any way. I had not satisfied my original mission in Korea, and it looked like I could get a second opportunity very soon.

Like Mr. Cowboy, my friend and the night clerk at the Royal Hotel in El Dorado, Kansas often said: "Timing has a lot to do with the outcome of a rain dance."

2. DEAR OL' MAUDE

Pfc. D.O. Brown was from Virginia Point, Texas, which he described as: "Two stores, two whores, and a black smith shop; world's coldest water and Nature's hottest women; catfish capital of the U.S.A." Right off the bat, D.O. had the big eye for Cpl. "Dear Ol' Maude," a darkroom technician who ran a section of the base photo lab where we often slept off the effects of the previous night's liberty in an unused photo darkroom laboratory. If someone wanted to use a dark room for official business, Cpl. Maude would direct those guys to another darkroom where we were not sleeping.

Cpl. Maude was a good ol' country gal and free spirit who had an apartment in Tijuana (say what!) Mexico, rode a big, burly Harley Davidson motor cycle hog that looked about twice her size, and often repeated her mantra: "Live hard, die young, and have a good-looking corpse." After knowing her less than two weeks, at age 19, she slammed her murder cycle full speed into a Mexican 18-wheel truck to complete her self-fulfilling prophecy.

The Marines who identified her mangled body in the Tijuana morgue said that she was not a good-looking corpse, and the Tijuana morgue worker bees tossed her dead body around like a discarded rag doll.

Talk about a life lesson. After visiting with her almost every day at the MCRD photo lab, we hardly knew her. Heck, D.O. hadn't even had a date with her yet. I imagine that he thought that he and she would be around a while longer for that, so he was waiting for payday to make the best possible impression.

There has to be a very insightful lesson in there somewhere. Maybe it was something simple like: "Don't drag race your monster Murder Cycle flat out on a Mexican highway in the middle of the night when snockered." Heck, I don't know.

3. INVOLUNTARY REFLEXES

The Duty Corporal at the MCRD Casual Company was a former pro-boxer and Korean combat veteran who had survived too many punches to his head, or else he was shell shocked after a year fighting on line in Korea. It had to be one or the other. The bunk next to mine was occupied by a very big, blond Pfc. from Utah who never rolled out immediately at reveille or for a night watch, and warned everyone that he could not help but involuntarily throw a flurry of punches in his sleep at anyone who touched him before he was fully awake. FYI: shaking his foot was the standard way of quietly wakening Marines in their bunks night or day.

One morning, the Duty Corporal shook the blond Pfc's foot when he had not hopped out of his rack quickly enough after reville. As he had predicted, the Pfc. did his "involuntary reflex" thing as he woke up, swinging both fists in a flurry of random knuckles. Purely by reflex, the ex-pro-boxer defended himself by knocking the Pfc. back onto his pillow and out like Lottie's left eye with one punch right between the pfc.'s eyes.

A-danged-mazingly, after that one incident, that Pfc. was no longer bothered by that troublesome, uncontrollable, involuntary, reflex when awakened by shaking his foot. Isn't that usually the way those reflex gigs work out?

Twenty years later, an eight-year old neighborhood kid repeatedly smacked my 8-year old son Davy or one of his sand-pile friends with some toy like a plastic rifle, hockey stick, whiffle ball bat, etc. and then ran home for lunch. Concerned, I told his dad, a grade school teacher, about that problem and the probability of serious injuries if that horse hockey continued. That teacher/dad apologized and said that he was sorry, but he also said that he could not control his own kid. So finally after weeks of that horse manure, I had a second friendly conversation with that brat's dad after his kid again hit several of the neighborhood kids with a long-handled plastic toy in our big sand pile and then ran home at lunch time. That was when I assured the brat's dad that the next time his "uncontrollable kid" hit any of the neighborhood kids with anything that could hurt them, when I got home from work, I would smack the dad with the exact same thing that the brat had used on the other kids in the neighborhood.

Would you believe that brat's dad suddenly found the formerly illusive magic words to make his kid never do that hit-and-run joehootinanny again during the next five years before we moved to Texas? Isn't it amazing what a difference a few well-chosen words can do for the dad as well as the kid?

4. BOB HOPE'S RANCH

While we were jumping through a series of hoops to transition from common OCS candidates to the "Elite 12" (or whatever that hogwash was) enlisted candidates for Pensacola Flight School, another OCS candidate from Hutchinson, Kansas and I took a weekend off to hitch hike all the way around Los Angeles to Malibu Canyon where my buddy's divorced dad managed Bob Hope's ranch a couple of miles up the mountain road from that famously beautiful beach. Unfortunately, or maybe fortunately, Bob Hope was not at home during our unannounced visit to his guest house, so we did a few light shovel-ready grunt chores around the ranch to earn our keep, had a few hours of peaceful R&R in that gorgeous setting, and were then thoroughly pummeled by the infamous undertow waves in the cove at Malibu Beach.

Brutal for uninitiated flatlanders like us, those lovely rolling waves sucked us amateur skin divers from the top of the waves down quite a way to the rocky bottom and then scuffed us back and forth unmercifully against the boulders on the bottom as the tide rolled in and out. When we limped back to duty Monday morning all battered and bruised, we looked like we had lost a fight with a herd of gorillas. That was my first and last black eye, and my first and last dip into the cove at Malibu Beach.

Since Bob Hope was not at his ranch, we could not get his autograph. So I left a generalized "Lefty" logo just for mutual grins. What goes around comes around.

5. ADVANCED COMBAT TRAINING

The Advanced Combat School at Camp Pendleton, California, was like an extended camp out, only with big-bore rifles, 60mm and 81mm mortars, 30- and 50-caliber machine guns, flame throwers, Bangalore torpedoes, and other seriously lethal weapons like that. Having been well prepared by years of bunny rabbit hunting among the Osage Orange hedge rows of the Kansas plains, coyote drives across the Arkansas River flood plains, shooting running jack rabbits and coyotes while strapped on the forward gun deck of a fast moving dune buggy, sneaking close enough in snow while wearing moccasins to skewer an angry hawk with a bow and arrow (no kidding), again and again slipping into the Wichita East High School cafeteria past the old night watchman for midnight ice cream snacks while working on our after-dark sneaking techniques, light fingering watermelons from a fenced and guarded junkyard (and getting shot at with a shotgun when in the third grade), regularly peeking into a farm barn bordello on the edge of town (and getting shot at with the pimp's 12-gauge shotgun while cousin George Dunn and I were in the fifth grade), camping on the Walnut River near El Dorado, Kansas for more than a month in Junior College after abandoning my originally assigned living quarters because the really old landlady insisted that I be back in that old 1890s shack before 9 p.m. every night (which I never did), and stuff like that, I could have taught the advanced combat infantry (grunt) sneaking and snooping course without ever setting a boondocker on Camp Pendleton.

And since I had memorized the *USMC Landing Party Manual* in DI School, could shoot a rabbit running full speed over a bumpy plowed field at least in or near the eye or somewhere in its head with my Marlon lever-action .22-caliber rifle so as not to ruin the meat, regularly slept on the ground and could live for weeks on tap water and cold beans, was a two-year college letterman at defensive end and the Saturday night bouncer in a rough and tumble Kansas honkie tonk for a year and a half, I fully believed that I was preconditioned to fight the Korean/Chinese hoards and be fairly comfortable in the process.

However, I was not fully qualified as an Advanced Combat grunt until later when I was thoroughly trained in the hills and mountains of northern California by elements of the iconic 5th Marine Brigade while stationed at NAS Moffett Field.

6. EVEN MORE IQ TESTING

Our tour of duty at NAS El Toro was about two weeks long; give or take a few as we bounced around from pillar to post only to hurry up and wait some more. What the heck, since not in any specified pipeline right then anyway, some down time was a welcome diversion. The setup: take the flight physical (including the darned eye test again), retake the IQ test (the third time in less than a year; which was a huge advantage), and fill-out a whole gaggle of brand new paper work in triplicate.

Funny thing: every time I took an IQ test, my IQ of record jumped quite a bit. Could it be that I was getting smarter and even smarter every day? Not only no, but heck NO. A big part of that improvement had to come from becoming more and more comfortable with that kind of test, as well as learning how to take advantage of test-timing. Waste time and you will be in deep doo doo with the clock deadline, and your IQ will be officially listed a lot lower than it actually is…and there goes the fast-track to whatever. That's not real good for a one-tour Marine let alone a career Marine.

However, probably the most significant reason was that after each IQ test in the military, those of us who took the test would get together later and talk about the questions that each of us believed we had missed, and invariably somebody in the group who did not miss a particular question would explain why. Of course the exact wording of each of those questions always changed a bit, but the meat of the questions was always the same. Therefore, if we understood the basic concept of the question, the past questions were the keys to the present questions and higher scores.

Think of IQ testing like crossword puzzles; the more you do them, the better/"smarter" you are graded. What a crock. Like my dear old dad often said: "There is a trick to everything, whether digging a ditch or taking an IQ test."

For example, my first IQ test score back in Wichita was in the mid-120's out of a possible 161 or 162 (I forget which) even though I wasted time messing with the really hard questions so that the bell rang before I could get to some of the easier questions at the end of the test. However, that qualified me for Officers Candidate School (OCS) and I was okay with that.

My second IQ test score—the one in boot camp—was in the mid-130's even with that BAM lieutenant's rosy red lips momentarily scrambling my mental pots and pans during that critically timed test. I thought that grade was just grand, and by then I had discovered that score could open a few more doors that were previously closed. Oooo raaah!

My unexpected third IQ test in less than one year, which was at El Toro Marine Air Base, qualified me for Mensa (say what!), and apparently opened a few more of the otherwise closed doors in the Marine hierarchy. Undoubtedly, I had benefitted a lot from the first two IQ tests, and maybe I flipped a coin a little better that third time than before.

Like my Dad always said: "Anything worth doing is worth doing well," so I always gave my current project—whatever it was—my best shot. Of course, the question and answer rehashes with my buddies after those tests were huge advantages. Honestly, I figured that the Mensa grade was a darned good joke on the Marine paper shufflers because I was sure that I wasn't any smarter than when I took that very first IQ test.

Naturally, I was not about to mention that to anyone in the chain of command, because that Mensa grade opened doors that might not be opened otherwise. So what the heck, I ran with it.

If you are planning on joining the Marines, be sure to take an IQ test at least a couple of times before you enlist. This test is a bit different than any that you have taken before, so you need to understand what is going on so that you will be comfortable when you finally take it for your permanent Marine records. A high IQ grade, a healthy body and a good attitude when you enlist in the Marines will open doors to many opportunities that are not available to fellow Marines who have an average IQ listed on their permanent records. Semper fi.

7. FLIGHT PHYSICALS

With the flight test physical coming up, I figured that the color test would surely shut the door to Pensacola on me. But what the heck, I'd had a good run and I was ready for Korea anyway. Even down in the lower ranks where we lived, we were all pretty sure that the Korean War would flare up again, and I really wanted to get a piece of it. Unlike most of the other 11 candidates, I had not dreamed of being a Marine pilot since I was a little kid. I always wanted to be a mud Marine; a grunt with a snazzy dress-blue uniform stashed in my sea bag.

However, if the Korean War was really winding down, I decided to just go with the flow along the path of the least resistance, especially since the OCS option was temporarily closed due to overcrowding from a surge of college graduates. If that process led to Pensacola with me driving airplanes; that was okay with me. However, if it led to Korea with me finally getting even, that was okay too. Deal the cards and go for broke. The Devil was in the details, and I was in the Marines on the pointy end of the United States' best military spear.

Just before we began the flight physical, Pfc. Bill Crowley stopped by and asked me to take his blood pressure test for him. He assured me that he did not have high blood pressure (or he would not have been there in the first place), but he apparently had moments when he would temporarily spike upward due to stress, and he was fairly well stressed at that moment. So what the heck; why not? I agreed to take his test for him because each test was being conducted by a different corpsman so that those guys probably could not keep track of us very well. Possibly, all 12 of the Marine candidates looked the same to them in our green uniforms and tight jarhead haircuts.

Purely out of curiosity, I asked Bill what he would be doing while I was taking his blood pressure test, and he offered to take my color test. Bingo! Too often in the past, people blessed with a potful of money had inferred that I would never have the money to go to college, or to buy a decent car, or Sunday-go-to-meeting clothes, or whatever, and I had always told them to "hide and watch." So getting past a darned color test when I never had any trouble with colors before was just another silly, officious, nit-picking challenge to overcome. Marines are taught and encouraged to overcome obstacles. As a Marine, I was overcoming this stupid darned color chart obstacle, as I should have with that dumb right-handed M1 rifle qualification test. Gung ho, gang. Work together and lighten the load.

So we lined up, and I took and passed my blood pressure test with an almost perfect score just like I always did. Then I went back to the end of the line, and when I took the test the second time, I told the same corpsman that I was Pfc. Bill Crowley. Bill did the same for me on the color test. He went through as himself, and then he got right back in the line and said that he was Pfc. Dave Ferman. We were right; all Marines did look alike to those over-worked corpsmen. We all passed with flying colors even though I never did see those dull red/green colors the same as the rest of our group.

While we walked around the El Toro air base in a group every day, Pfc. George Bailey and I were kind of anxious about going home on our first leave. We knew that some of our now-semi-habitual Marine DI colorful (i.e., obscene) language was not appropriate for mixed company or talking to our mothers or future wives. So we mutually agreed to be more sensitive about our colorful if somewhat obscene language.

Therefore, if any of the guys in our group said anything that was not appropriate to say in front of our families or the good Sisters of St. Joseph, we would all stop and stomp our feet in righteous indignation. As we walked around the air base, I was surprised how often the entire group stopped and stomped their feet in righteous indignation while I would stop and wonder: "Gee whizz, what did I say this time."

That silly protocol was good practice and very necessary training before my first leave at home. But even then, I felt like an accident looking for a place to happen.

8. FINALLY HOME SWEET HOME

Back at home on leave in Wichita, I had to be very careful about my language which had become pretty darned colorful after boot camp and duty as a Marine DI. At the dinner table, I had to carefully review everything that I said before saying it. For example: "Please pass the bread" instead of "Pass the frig'n bread, dammit." That was a huge challenge, but I thought that I was making progress until Mrs. and Mr. Vann invited me to have supper with their whole family. In high school, Mr. Vann was our assistant baseball coach in the Summer League, and a big booster for our high school team where their son, Richard Leon Patrick (Buddy) Vann, played third base and I started and played right field because I could only go about seven innings while recovering from that worse head injury.

Mrs. Vann was always in the stands either watching the games or chaperoning us during traveling games throughout the state of Kansas, and once for a whole week in Denver where we played and won the first interstate Little League baseball title after WWII. Their oldest daughter, Beverly Jean Vann, and I went through 12 years of grade and high school together. She was a shy, modest but really good looking little blond girl. That probably should have led to something, but nobody in our family had a car, and I didn't think she would go on a date riding on the bus, or the handle bars of my very old, gut-shot bicycle, or my gutless Cushman motor scooter. Also, I had to work every day and most evenings so Beverly and I were just very good friends who had seen a lot of each other down through the years. Then there were the two very young Vann girls who I could not recognize if I met them in a phone booth.

Back at the supper table at the Vann's home, I was doing pretty good overall with my colorful, salty dog Marine language by thinking of every word before I said it, and then white washing each sentence so it would be acceptable in that very special company. However, someone at the table asked me off the cuff if I had seen Bruce Nobles, a mutual friend who had been our catcher on our summer baseball teams. Before I could clean up my act, I blurted: "Oh. That shit bird," and everything came to a screeching halt.

I was so darned embarrassed. I just sat there in the thunderous silence and stared at a big platter full of boiled shrimp in the middle of the table directly in front of me. I can still see that huge pile of shrimp even to this day, and I don't remember how we got through the rest of that meal, but we did.

Traditionally, when I ate supper with the Vanns, I would either wash or dry the dishes after supper, and Mrs. Vann or Beverly would handle the other half of the task while we talked. That night, I did the dish washing, but in an awkward silence. Finally, in my embarrassment I blurted out my apology to Mrs. Vann by saying: "Gosh Mrs. Vann. I am so sorry. I really fucked up."

Years later when Buddy Vann got married, I was the professional although free photographer for that event. Although I had never seen Mrs. Vann take a sip of beer, wine or any other kind of tanglefoot, after everyone else had gone home, Mrs. Vann and I sat side-by-side at the main table with a bottle of some kind of popskull and we toasted almost everyone we both knew. Mrs. Vann was one grand lady. Over the years, she cut me a lot of slack, and I loved her and Mr. Vann a lot.

9. U.S. MARINE QUOTE

Back in the early 1930s during the "Banana Wars" in Nicaragua, Captain (later Major General) Lewis "Chesty" Puller, was discussing guerrilla war tactics with a number of mid-grade army officers who would be the future U.S. Army generals in WW II. When the limited scope of the skirmishes in the jungle came into question, Chesty said and I quote: "Well, it ain't much of a war, but it's the only war we've got." Oooooh rahhh!

VI. NAS MOFFETT FIELD

Ode to the BAR—the Browning automatic rifle—my favorite Grunt infantry weapon which I almost mastered. Sing to the tune of "Bless Them All."

"Bless them all, bless them all,
The AP, the tracer, the ball,* *(types of ammunition)
Push on the change lever,
Pull back on the bolt,
Squeeze on the trigger
And wait for the jolt.

Oh it kicks like a Model T Ford,
And death is its only reward.
And when you are deadd,
Some other Jarheadd,
Will pick up the BAR you adore."

That's all that I remember, but don't forget, that was 65 long years ago.

1. CPL. TILLERY

On my first day at NAS Moffett Field, I was looking for a decent bunk, and Cpl. Tillery gave me his because he was going home to Muskogee, Oklahoma on his first leave after recovering from too many months on the front lines in Korea. When I saw him again a month later as he returned to Moffett, he had a big cloth bandage wrapped around his head like a swami from India. When I asked him what happened, he said and I quote: "I really don't know. I was sitting in this crappy old honkie-tonk nightclub back home, throwing a few empty beer bottles on the stage while some boney old stripper was floppin' around, and some S.O.B. came up behind me and hit me with a sap full of steel B.Bs. Hell's bells, I don't know why."

The funny part is that Cpl. Tillery really did not seem to know why anybody should have taken offense at him just for tossing a few empty beer bottles in the general direction of some bony, old stripper. He really did need to get a bit more civilized around those raunchy Oklahoma road houses outside of Muskogee. Some of those grungy old gals may have been somebody's mama or, more likely, a common law "old lady" with the club bouncer or somebody like that.

2. CLUE TO A LONG FOOTBALL SEASON

Later the first day after I was settled in the Marine barracks at NAS Moffett Field, the football coach and a trainer took me over to the practice field, issued my practice gear, a game uniform, a play book, and penciled me in at left defensive end, punter and point-after-touchdown kicker for the game on the following weekend. I only had three days to practice with those guys before the first kickoff.

My first football game with the Red Raiders was against the Stanford University Cardinal's second team. During the first quarter, I got tired of bouncing off a much larger, pretty darned decent tight end straight in front of me, so I moved about half a position to my right and split the gap between that end and their tackle. Apparently, each of those guys thought that the other guy was supposed to block me, so in their confusion I popped into the Stanford backfield untouched and smeared Stanford's star halfback, Al Napoleon, head-on for at least a five-yard loss. Gasping for breath, Napoleon did not get up very quickly. In fact, he lay right there for a few minutes while their trainer got a workout. Our home crowd of sailors and Marines went crazy, and the Navy Wave cheerleaders joyfully shook their pompoms and anything else that they had to shake in wild celebration.

However, the next thing that I knew, a substitute defensive end ran onto the field, took my place and I left the field somewhat bewildered. You see, our coach, who I understand had been the former football coach at Annapolis sometime before that, jerked me off the field and chewed me loud and clear for "being out of position" from the way he had drawn the "X's" and "O's" for his defensive team.

That's when I knew that we were in for a long season. When football coaches are demoted from a national powerhouse like Annapolis and sent to a cobbled together military team like NAS Moffett Field, there had to be a darned good reason for it, and I believed that I had solved that mystery in my very first game. Our head coach was a master of the "X's" and "O's," but he did not understand defensive football, especially from the prospective of his defensive ends.

Incidentally, about two months later I sat in the stands and watched Al Napoleon score the winning touchdown against U.C. Berkley, which I believe eventually earned Stanford the Pac 8 championship that year. You wouldn't think that the Stanford varsity used us as an extra warmup game for the "Big Kids" would you? Hey, we didn't lose by much. Stanford was a darned good college team in 1953, and apparently our Navy/Marine Red Raiders weren't too bad either despite our thickheaded, hidebound, head coach. At least he was a semi-likeable old goat once I got to know him.

3. FORT ORD

By the time we tangled with Fort Ord at their field, I was playing some offensive end, quite a lot of defensive end, punter and PAT kicker. I believe that Fort Ord's right defensive tackle was the 1952 All-American defensive tackle from Oklahoma. A monster disguised as a future NFL announcer, this guy was much taller than me, had forearms as big as my thighs, not much neck and a leg on each corner. I thought that I would probably die right there on that field that night, but if so, I decided that I would die like a good Marine facing the enemy.

But surprisingly, on the very first play I blocked him and darned if I didn't move him out of his position (say what?). On the next couple of plays, I moved him again and again. Pretty soon, silly me, I figured that I had this guy's number, and in the next huddle I told our quarterback to run the ball to my side of the line of scrimmage if he wanted to make some easy yardage into their secondary.

That was a big mistake because for about four or five plays, that All-American tackle showed me why he was an All-American and why I was not. He beat the bejabbers out of me without hardly breaking a sweat. After that, we both took it a little easier on the other since he was saving himself for professional football and later stardom as a football announcer, and I was just trying to make it through all four quarters alive. Pain hurts. I'm not sure now, but I believe that we won, but not by very much.

It was mildly consoling to know that in a shootout with M1 rifles at 500 yards, I would clean that All-American's clock every day and every way.

4. PREMO NAVY CHOW

Naval Air Station (NAS) Moffett Field was rated the best chow in the U.S. Navy that year. Where other bases or ships might allow each sailor a small eight-ounce cardboard container of milk with each meal (or less), the chow hall at Moffett had a bunch of huge, shiny, steel containers with beer bar type spigots with which we could take all of the icy cold milk that we could drink; and we did that over and over again. Uncharacteristically for the Navy, at each meal the cooks served several kinds of meat, vegetables, desserts, etc. and we could take our choice or else pile some of everything on our trays, then go back for seconds or even thirds.

Moffett Field was the Navy re-enlistment paradise where sailors from marginal, remote bases in the Pacific Ocean like Guam or some similar sandy hell hole were assigned just before their enlistments were over. The Navy's apologetic story: we are so sorry that you great guys were assigned to such a terrible place as Guam (or wherever). Moffett

Field is what the real Navy is like, so please think again about re-enlisting for another adventurous four years.

Likewise, the Marine gate guards and MP motor patrols were instructed not to be too strict with these sailors even if they returned from San Francisco or San Jose snockered, wearing non-regulation argyle sox and even if their uniforms were on basackwards. We would still pick them up on liberty and bring them back to the base for various infractions, but we dropped them off at their barracks and not the base brig. I liked that a lot better than the way we handled that situation before.

However, when some of them took the bait and re-enlisted, they were often shipped right back to Guam or one of those other fly speck islands in the middle of the vast Pacific Ocean. Who can you trust? Certainly not the U.S. Navy cooks and bakers who piled on the food to overflowing and never stopped smiling because they knew what was going on. Of course, the real S.O.B.s were the two-faced Navy personnel pukes who were talking out of both sides of their mouths. There were two things that I could not stand about those pukes, and that was each one's face.

5 "PERMANENT PFC." ELADIO GONZALES

Although not the best barracks Marines, permanent Pfc. Eladio "Gunny" Gonzales and the rest of the 5th Marine Brigade, 1st Marine Division of "Frozen Chosin Reservoir" fame, were the best Marines that I ever saw in the field. During a number of company-sized training maneuvers in the hills bordering the future Silicone Valley, they could all run full bore with their heads much lower than me, transition from maneuver to coordinated, directed-fire faster and smoother than anyone I had previously known, and had returned to California armed with the new U.S. Army M2 carbines although the Marines were issued only the older M1 carbines at that time.

These guys were not just good, they were very good at many things that would keep you alive in combat. I saw several guys who put 17 out of 20 BAR rounds through a bunker slit at about 200 yards in short bursts. That's damn fine shooting. I sure as heck couldn't do it.

The two following sea stories are not mine, but they are too good to be ignored, so I will make an exception to the usual rule that sea stories must be about the teller in some way. Anyway, according to several veterans of the Fighting 5th Marines, Eladio made "permanent Pfc." when ordered to train a Navy Corpsman to survive in Korea by clearing a jammed BAR so that the corpsman could fire it to defend himself because the North Koreans and ChiComs considered our corpsmen to be easy targets. However, Eladio was using someone else's weapon (the Browning Automatic Rifle is a 30-caliber rifle-like machinegun) or, more likely, a float BAR from the battlefield that had no particular owner to clean it at that particular time.

The BAR is ready to fire when the bolt is fully aft rather than forward like most rifles. So when Eladio cleared the vertically held weapon by banging its butt plate on the ground according to the Standard Operating Procedure (SOP), the mud-caked sear (say what!) in the owner-less BAR released the bolt, it slid forward and fired a round, then slid aft but would not engage the muddy sear again, so the bolt slid forward again and again, etc., until all 20 rounds in the magazine were fired straight up at the sky. That burst cut the main support structure of the collapsing squad tent as Eladio hung on to the bucking BAR to keep it firing vertically so that no one inside the tent would be accidentally shot.

Unfortunately, a new Commanding Officer, who was, I believe, a reserve artillery officer rather than an infantry officer, did not know boo doodly about the BAR (which is hard to believe, but who knows during a war), and busted Eladio down to a "permanent Pfc." at the disciplinary hearing. I guess that cannon cocker had never fired a BAR before. Apparently, Eladio was stuck with that recruit training "No excuse, Sir" response, and was not allowed to defend himself because if he had, I would have bet that Eladio would have beaten those idiotic charges at a fair hearing.

Eladio certainly had a way with words and, as sworn by his comrades, in combat, you could not find a better Marine than Eladio Gonzales. He should have gotten a commendation for quick thinking rather than a demotion, and every enlisted grunt in his unit darned well knew it for sure.

Every enlisted Marine that I knew at Moffett still called Eladio "Gunny," which stood for Gunny Sgt. (i.e., three stripes up and two more stripes down).

6. WELL-ARMED ROBBERY

As long as we're on the subject of my good friend and actual blood brother, Eladio Gonzales; many of the veterans of the 5th Marines told me the same story so I'm pretty darned sure that it is true. After about a year of grubbing around in the mud and fighting darned near every day, one afternoon Eladio and another grunt mud Marine walked about two miles to the rear to an Army Officers' mess tent that had crystal glasses, fine china, linen table cloths, real silverware, a white-coated mess crew, and adult beverages (near the MLR in Korea, no less).

As the story goes, Eladio and his buddy walked into that big officer's mess tent between meals, confronted the mess crew, and declared a robbery. In the middle of all of that Army opulence, Eladio and his buddy would settle for nothing less than a case of whisky fifths.

Somehow, the Army guys did not believe Eladio was serious, so he shot up the top of the tent with his BAR to make his point. Eladio and his buddy then took off for the Marine MLR (i.e., main line of resistance) toting a case of blue-ribbon whisky between them. Predictably but unfortunately, they stopped in the middle of a remote rice paddy, got snockered, passed out and were found by USMC MPs who punished them in the worst way they possibly could; they took both Marines back to the front lines to continue their share of the war.

In war, two top-notch, proven Marine grunts are worth how many brig rats? Check the math.

7. GREEN MARINES

I did not understand the occasional high-level discrimination in the Marine Corps at that time since all enlisted Marines, whether white/black/Indian/Mexican/Samoan/Oriental/etc. extraction were "Green

Marines" to each other. Eladio's citation for bravery clearly stated that he and his patrol were ambushed in Korea by Chinese troops, and pinned down under heavy fire. One Marine was badly wounded. During an extended defensive battle from shell holes well forward of the Marine MLR and running low on ammo, Eladio carried his wounded buddy back to our lines under intense fire. Apparently, the Marines fighting at the MLR were also heavily engaged, so Eladio loaded up with an extra BAR and all of the ammo bandoliers and hand grenades that he could carry, crawled back to the battle in the shell holes, and laid down a base of fire with his BAR so that his patrol could move back to the Marine MLR. Then, after dark, Eladio tossed his last couple of grenades, and then snuck back to our MRL under heavy fire. For this heroic action, he was awarded the Letter of Commendation with Combat "V."

Say what! Eladio should have received at least the Silver Star medal. A-danged-mazing! Was that stupid reserve artillery officer still in command?

I remember the exact words of Eladio's commendation because a group of his combat buddies and I held an informal re-presentation formation where a dozen or so enlisted Marines stood at attention in formation while I read the commendation word for word in a loud command-presence voice, and then rendered faux cheek-kissing honors much like the friggin' French Foreign Legion.

Lately, I have seen a number of WW II, Korean War and Vietnam War service men finally awarded medals that they should have been received when they were on active duty. While they are at it, someone with appropriate influence should look up Pfc. Eladio Gonzales and give him the awards that we all knew he so richly deserved. After more than a year on line fighting the North Korean and Chinese bad guys, I believe that Eladio received only the Korean Theatre ribbon with several battle stars, the Purple Heart, that Letter of Commendation with Combat V, the UN ribbon and of course the National Defense ribbon.

I know of Army guys who were in the First Gulf War and came back with up to eight ribbons and awards for that 100-hour blitzkrieg, and then had to be treated for battle fatigue on top of that. Then there was those three Army cowboys who were captured by the Serbs outside of

Kosovo. They were each awarded at least six ribbons including a Purple Heart for bruises (say what!) when they were beaten up after they were captured while horsing around and actually playing silly games with their new Humvee vehicle with mounted 50-calibre machine gun.

Give us a break. That pig is still a pig no matter how much lip stick they put on it.

8. CPL. HOOKER

Cpl. Hooker was a Marine's Marine. At least five veterans of the 5th Marines each told me how Cpl. Hooker found himself masked from the battle by a terrain anomaly as seemingly all of the Chinese grunts in Korea were advancing across a valley toward his position on a hill. So while his buddies poured fire at the Chinese from within their bunkers or their sandbagged fighting holes, Cpl. Hooker stood up in his fighting hole so he could see better, and calmly fired round after round of aimed fire into the onrushing Chinese hordes. What a guy!

His buddies in Korea also told me that Cpl. Hooker was afraid of frogs. When I doubted that, they told me to go ask him if I did not believe them. So I did. In response Hooker said: "Yeah, heck yes; I'm afraid of frogs." I asked him why, adding a flippant: "Heck, they can't bite you, can they?" Hooker looked at me like I was a slow learner and replied: "They have a mouth, don't they?

9. PING PONG CHAMPION

Cpl. Hooker had been the California ping pong champion before the Korean Conflict (who was it that said "conflict" instead of "war"? It certainly wasn't anybody who was ducking incoming fire, pooping in a slit trench and eating C rations). Anyway, I thought that I was a pretty good ping pong player, but Hooker initially beat me like a drum. However, I got better and better every time I played him so that fairly soon I was beating everyone else on the base who would take a bet, but not Hooker. My old Dad often said: "It is always good to have a goal."

One morning, Hooker and I were scheduled to play a game of ping pong down in the Rec Room, but Hooker begged off because he was definitely ill, was running a fever and needed to go to sick bay eee-mediately if not sooner. Recognizing the opportunity, I whined about my missing something or other that was very special in order to play that game, and nagged him until he finally agreed to play one game before going to sick bay. Long story short, I finally beat him, but just barely. Of course, a few days later Hooker recovered and he beat me soundly once again. However, I can still say in all candor that I have beaten the former California ping-pong champ.

The devil is often in the details.

10. PFC. (LATER COLONEL) GEORGE BAILEY

My pal, Pfc. George Bailey had a brand new Oldsmobile coupe that he bought with cash after just one summer of running the snow cone concession at his families' fishing lodge at Possum Kingdom Lake back in Texas. I thought that sounded like a pretty good deal to me, but George confided to me in all seriousness: "That's not good work for a man." Of course, he said that while driving his new Oldsmobile coupe that I could not afford. I had worked the prior summer in the oil patch doing "men's work" for just "walking-around money," so his lesson fell on deaf ears.

Although we were all former college guys and very healthy athletes, we never did get to first base with the serious, female workaholic students at nearby Stanford University. Of course, that was an ongoing frustration until I found our former high-school quarterback, Jack Gebert, at the Fiji Fraternity house. He told me that although he was the first-string quarterback at Stanford at that time while the original quarterback was mending from some kind of broken body part, and he was also the pledge father for one of Bing Crosby's boys (and Jack was a very good-looking guy with lots of money to spend), even he had a hard time getting dates on the Stanford campus.

Connecting the dots, we saw the light, gave up on nearby Stanford and moved our base of coed operations to the University of California at

Berkley, which was way to heck and gone over the bridge into Oakland on the far side of San Francisco, then a few miles north to Berkley.

Like they said: "If you can't score at Berkley, you might as well join the monks because you can't score anywhere. Do I hear an "Aaaa-men" from the peanut gallery?

11. UNPARALLED PLUPERFECT PRIDE

The 5th Marine veterans of "Frozen Chosin Reservoir" fame were a proud group of proven warriors. During an overly long-winded change-of-command ceremony at NAS Moffett, we stood at parade rest for about an hour in the relatively hot California sunshine while wearing winter-service green wool uniforms. One big, husky Marine veteran, Cpl. Baker I think it was, finally said to heck with it, he was going to fall out and watch the ceremony from the beckoning shade of a First Aid shelter nearby. However, his buddies reminded him that at least one sailor had to fall out first to uphold Marine honor. So Cpl. Baker was on standby to standby.

Eventually, a tiny blond Navy Wave passed out in an adjacent formation. Immediately, Cpl. Baker whispered: "That's it. Here I go," followed by the loud clattering sound of his M1 rifle falling on the asphalt parade ground. "I'm right behind you," and Cpl. Sanchez's M1 clattered on the asphalt as he too went down rather dramatically. Within minutes, there were maybe six or so 5th Marine veterans sitting in the shade of that First Aid shelter, sipping cold drinks and having their faces wiped with cold wet towels by compassionate young nurses while they enjoyed their front row seats for the rather elaborate and overly long ceremony.

But think about the irony of the moment. The honor of those battle-proved Marine warriors was upheld by a sick little 100-pound Navy Wave office pinkie. I loved it.

I was holding the U.S. flag as the lead element of the color guard, so there was no way that I could join the smiling Marines sitting in the shade and laughing about my bad luck. However, I had put a lot of bee's wax inside the creases of my wool trousers so that when a hot iron was applied to the outer side, that crease was so rock solid that I could move my knees back and forward but nobody could know the difference. When my legs were "at ease," my trousers were still at attention.

12. PFC. (LATER LT. COL.) JOE D. BOLLING

My good friend, Pfc. Joe D. Bolling and I were like two peas in a pod. We were both young Marines; 6 feet, 3 inches tall; weighed about 220 pounds; had dark brown hair; took a lot of time off from formal duty to play football and basketball on Moffett teams; were initially awaiting transfer to OCS and then later to pilot training at Pensacola. Most of the 5th Marine veterans at Moffett Field continually got Joe D. ("Jody") and yours truly mixed up as if we were twins. Finally, I got a taste of that mixup when the Marine Detachment was ordered by the Navy's new base Commanding Officer to return our dress shoe color from much-shinier black to the official cordovan color, and then he scheduled a re-inspected for the next morning.

So I stayed up much of the night after an extended liberty in San Jose, removed the black color with cigarette lighter fluid and steel wool, and re-stained, buffed, and then spit shined every centimeter of those shoes to a high cordovan gloss. They were, indeed, things of beauty.

Still exhausted and hurting for sleep when reveille blew at 05:30, I was just reaching for my newly shined shoes when Joe D. crawled down from the top bunk, said "Thank you, Dave," put those shoes on, and hustled off to breakfast. I had cleaned and spit shined Joe's dress shoes that were the exact same 11 ½ D size as mine. Needless to say, I had to miss breakfast to prepare my own shoes for the onrushing 09:00 inspection. Of course, I did not have time for the first-class spit shine like I had applied on Jody's shoes, but that swabby Navy base C.O. did not notice the difference.

I felt darned lucky that MSgt. Ramsey from DI School did not conduct that inspection. I would have been in a heap of trouble, and probably would not see a liberty pass for the rest of that year because, excuse wise, that old dog would not hunt. I kid you not.

13. MASTER SGT. O'DAY

Master Sgt. O'Day had been in the Marines more than 32 years (his final enlistment was extended at the start of the Korean War), and he never let anyone forget it. One day, he sent a corporal with some kind of a request to a Navy squadron for some reason, and the salty old Master Chief over there got hyper and threw the corporal out of his office. Infuriated, O'Day called that Navy Chief on the phone to straighten him out. I could only hear O'Day's side of the conversation, which went something like this: "Listen up, Chief. You're not messin' with no dammed "boot" here. I've been in my U.S. Marine Corp for 32 dad-blamed years." There was a pause while the chief spoke, and then O'Day said: "Oh yeah. Is that so? And what month did you join, Chief?" There was another pause while the chief spoke again, and then O'Day bellowed into the phone: "April! Well I joined in March, you damned BOOT! So don't you ever give any one of my Marines that load of crap again! DO...YOU...HEAR...ME?"

After 32 years, just one month's seniority still held its authority in Master Sgt. O'Day's Old Corps world.

About 24 years later, I learned that a good friend, John Cochran, who worked on the same program at LTV, had joined the Marines in Phoenix, Arizona, on the exact same day that I joined the Marines in Kansas City. However, my Marine serial number is 10 numbers lower than his serial number. Therefore, for 34 years until John passed away, I laughingly called my good buddy Marine a "boot" whenever he and I were on different sides of the fence about anything. That always clouded our occasional arguments, but it certainly added a skochi bit of continuity.

14. SGT. LEMAN BRIGHTMAN

Sgt. Leman Brightman (a future Ph.D Professor of Indian Affairs and an occasional TV commentator) was a full-blooded Sioux Indian from Oklahoma, a Korean vet, and our best fullback on the base football team. Physically impressive, Brightman was built like a Greek god statue on a museum pedestal; stood about 6 feet and 4 inches tall, and was as muscular as a professional body builder. On the other hand, Pfc. Kenny Spotted Bear from the Sioux Reservation in Montana was a short, squat, 17-year old man-child and the most inquisitive and naïve person I have ever met. We called Kenny "Spots" for short, and he seemed to like that nickname so it stuck.

One day in the barracks, Sgt. Brightman had just taken a shower and was wearing only his boxer shorts in the barracks when he said to Spots: "All Sioux are big like me" as he flexed his well-muscled body like a showoff body builder at Muscle Beach. "So what are you Spots; a Mexican?"

With his mouth shut tighter than a bull's lips at fly time, Spots sullenly and uncharacteristically said nothing in response, and that continued when he and I soon went on guard duty at a remote gate on the far side of the field where aircraft passed very close overhead as they took off or landed. However, after about an hour of total and absolutely unusual silence, Spotted Bear abruptly said: "Brightman's not so big." Amused, I told Spots that I thought Brightman looked pretty doggone big to me. Then, I asked Spots if he knew anyone bigger than Brightman. Spots thought a moment and then said: "Yes I do. Sylvester One Skunk and Charlie Yellow Horse are bigger than Brightman." Then after an agonizingly long pause, Spots added: "But Charlie Yellow Horse is in San Quentin. He don't come home no more."

After that, Spots sullenly did not say another word during the remainder of the four-hour gate watch. That was really unusually because normally he would bang my ears for the whole four-hour watch when he would ask simple questions such as: "If that airplane over there would come straight at us, what would you do?" I would respond with some simple answer like "I would jump in that ditch," and then, invariably, Spots would say: "Why." Normally, he could keep that up for the entire four-hour watch, then keep it going on the Jeep ride back to the barracks, and then in the barracks as well. I guess that I should have counted my many blessings as they say; "count them one by one." Spots had a lot of reservation smarts like: "Never kick a fresh cow pie on a hot day," but he did not know beans from buckshot when it came to city boy smarts.

15. COLD SHOWER TAP DANCE

One night as I was sobering up in the potty/shower room of the huge USO in San Jose, I noticed below the shower door that a fully dressed Marine in winter green woolen uniform and dazzling spit-shined shoes was showering. Curious, I opened the door to the shower and found Sgt. Brightman holding a passed out but also fully dressed Kenny Spotted Bear up to the running shower nozzle, which was soaking both of them. Brightman looked at me very seriously for several seconds, and then he proclaimed in all seriousness: "Doggone Indians. Can't drink whisky worth a damn."

16. SHE LED, I FOLLOWED.

I think it was the next evening in the USO when I came in the front door and noticed a very pretty girl sitting at a table all alone while all of the other gals (maybe 30 or more) were dancing with the visiting service men. That was really unusual because the local gals came to the USO to dance. Later, when I came out of the large, luxurious potty and shower room and was headed back to the base, I could not help but notice that the same pretty girl was still sitting alone watching all of the other girls dance. What the heck was going on? I had to know.

So I walked over to the young lady, introduced myself and asked her if she would care to dance. She said "Sure" and began to get up, and she got further up, and finally she was towering over me like Wilt Chamberland. Remember, I was 6 feet and 3 inches tall. However, I only came up to her nose. And when we started to slow dance, it was kind of like dancing with a telephone pole. I could not move her. Finally I asked her if she would like to lead. She perked up, smiled and said: "I usually do," and she did. I have forgotten her name, but I certainly would have loved to have had her on my coed volleyball team when I got back to college.

17. WE LOST, I WON.

Our NAS Moffett Field Red Raiders football team was pretty decent, but not very deep. In fact, we were not deep at all, especially at fullback. Sgt. Leman Brightman was it. But that had not been a problem during the regular season since Sgt. Brightman was a horse of a man. A former first-string fullback on the Oklahoma A&M Aggies team before the Korean War, he ran through, around and over some of the best defensive teams in college and the Armed Forces football teams as well. He was essentially our whole ground game with a bit of help from two minor league halfbacks and a nice guy, but not an exceptional quarterback. With Brightman in the game, our opponents had to set up tight against a darned good running game while at the same time they had to stay honest and spread out to defend our usually short to medium distance passing game.

That quandary kept our opponents guessing, and quite often they zigged when they should have zagged, and we did quite well in the confusion. If we had the football inside the other team's 10-yard line, Brightman would score. Take it to the bank. He definitely would score no matter what.

In fact, we were favored to win a nationally televised Armed Forces Game of the Week with the San Francisco State team that had apparently played well over their heads all season just like we had. We were looking forward to the chance to show off in front of a national audience. Even my Mom, who never cared one whit for football when I was in high school and college, went next door to a neighbor lady's house to watch the game on TV with her friends back in Wichita. Mom did not get a TV until 1962.

Unfortunately, only a couple of days before the big game, Sgt. Brightman fell down the side of a deep, steep gully and was badly injured when we were on maneuvers in the mountains north of San Jose. By game time, he could not walk without crutches. We were in deep doo doo with our running game a mere shadow of what it had been all year. We had no viable replacement for Brightman, and without a decent running game, SF State could lay back and shut down our passing game with ease. But the game had to be played, and we showed up to give it our best shot, which was not good enough.

Basically, the game boiled down to SF State kicking the ball to us, we would cobble together three plays, and then I would punt that darned ball as far and as high as I could on a breeze-less day. Then our defense would get the ball back, we would run three more plays and I would again punt that darned ball as far and as high as I could. Under those conditions, there were no finesse kicks to go out of bounds inside their 20-yard line or any other fancy joehootinanny like that. Almost all of my many punts all afternoon were from deep in our own territory. Like I said, there was almost no breeze and all my punts were over 50 yards in the air and several were around 60 yards (40 to 50 yards on the ground). SF State had no runbacks against me because with those long hang times, our speedy ends and halfbacks got downfield and would be standing there with the SF State receivers waiting to pounce when my punts came down.

Since I kick left footed and apparently those SF State punt receivers had not practiced catching punts with a left-footed spin, so their receivers had a heck of a time handling several of those punts. In fact, one got away and we pounced on it deep in their territory. We still could not muster a touchdown without Brightman on the field, but I got a field goal that was barely longer than a point-after-touchdown so at least we were not skunked. I don't remember the score, but I think it was something like 14 to 3, which was not bad under such adverse conditions.

That was a terrible, frustrating game for us, but my Mom back in Kansas loved every minute of it because the TV announcer was constantly saying nice things about her son's punting on national TV. I did all of our kicking except for the opening kickoff. I also had a pretty good game at defensive end so my number came up fairly regularly. We did not have our names on our backs back then.

In the end, everything turned out okay because in the months following that game, I received about a dozen offers for football scholarships from major universities all over the United States. I think that the announcer must have mentioned that I still had two years of college eligibility remaining. Like a dummy, I automatically threw away every offer from east of the Mississippi River or west of the Rocky Mountains, and kept those from Kansas, Kansas State, Oklahoma A&M, Nebraska, Arkansas and Denver University in my sea bag.

Of course, I picked the wrong school for the wrong reason, but that's another story for another time.

18. "SEA DADDY'S" VIP

Ed "Sea Daddy" Somebody, one of the sailors on our football team, was also a designated driver for visiting dignitaries and other VIPs like that. Late one night on the midnight-to-4-a.m. watch at the main gate, I saw Sea Daddy returning a base car and stopped him to shoot the breeze for a minute since it had been an unusually uneventful night. Sea Daddy did not say a word, but motioned towards the back seat with his head while clearing his throat a couple of times. When I finally got his drift and looked into the deep shadow of the back seat, all I could see was a mass of a dark Navy blue officer's coat with a white shirt collar and three or four stars disappearing under the lapel.

Caught off guard, I put out the forbidden cigarette in the palm of my left hand as I snapped to attention and saluted smartly with my right hand. More than 65 years later, I still have a faint scar on my left palm to remind me of one of the many dangers of smoking.

Like my buddy Bill Brill's mom often said: "Pain hurts."

19. PFC. CAVENAUGH'S NEAT MOM

After being plied all evening with too-much hard liquor by Pfc. Francis Cavenaugh's old Irish mama, who incidentally was a San Francisco city librarian and looked exactly like an old Irish librarian mama from Central Casting in the movies. She was short, a bit plump, cheerful as the dickens, and apparently ageless. The bottomless drinks she served us were anything but chintzy, and even the salad had popskull sprinkled over it. I thought that I had died and staggered to heaven. Mama Cavenaugh was my kind of chef.

After our visit and feeling no pain, Pfc. Bill Crowley (a future vice president or maybe president of a Blue Cross division) and I were delivered by her comparatively tea-totaler other son to the Marine Memorial Hotel in downtown San Francisco. No sooner had his car pulled away from the curb, we both got tanglefooted, fell into the gutter at the main entrance, and lay head-to-head at ease while still talking to each other about getting up and moving on. Bill and I each thought that the other guy should rise up like a Phoenix and drag the other guy away from that uncomfortable gutter. Unfortunately, neither of us packed the gear to get up and do the deed, so we just laid there discussing current events.

Finally, we were both dragged out of the gutter, brushed off and deposited in the hotel potty and shower room by the doorman and several passing Marines who were also concerned that we could get squashed by the many taxi cabs pulling up to the curb at the front door. That thought had crossed my mind as well, but there was nothing I could do about it in that condition since that darned Bill Crowley would not get up, pick me out of that nasty gutter and get me up to that famous Semper Fi Bar on the 13th floor.

Looking back, I wish that I had a dime for every dime I spent in that fine and famous bar.

20. THE INFAMOUS RATHSKELLER BAR

As a 6-foot, 3-inch tall, 220-pound, clean shaven, under-aged but thirsty thrill seeker who spent many Saturday evenings in the Rathskeller basement bar at the University of California in Berkley for several months, I used one of Bill Crowley's friendly Sigma Chi's ID cards which identified me as Tony somebody the VI (junior to the what power?) from some place in Florida.

As I recall, Tony the Sixth was described on his ID card as being something like 5 feet and 4 inches tall and weighed all of 120 pounds or so with a paving stone in each pocket. I believe that he had a sharp shaped face, piercing eyes and a Van Dyke beard. I mention that because I was carded every weekend as I entered the Rathskeller bar, but I was never refused entrance. I think that the hippy dippy gate keeper was usually stoned by the time that he showed up for work with his eyeballs focused about on Europe.

Welcome to Berkley, California. Anything goes and probably will.

21. RHEA'S WRATH

At the Rathskeller Bar one Saturday evening, Bill Crowley pointed out a strikingly attractive, semi-amazon, graduate-student/football groupie/golden girl named Rhea who was cavorting with a gaggle of English majors in a nearby booth. Right out of the gate, that was no problem despite our age difference. She was only seven or eight very good years older than me. Always a positive guy, Bill was positive that Rhea was the girl that I should marry; "the sooner the quicker." That sounds pretty ridiculous now, but Rhea had seen me play football on national TV and somebody said that she liked the cut of my jib, whatever the heck that meant. Anyway, that was a good start for this hick from the sticks.

Mea culpa, mea culpa, mea maxima culpa with bells on.

After a couple of hours of getting acquainted in the booth in the back in the corner in the dark, Rhea and I had gotten somewhat snockered on several pitchers of Bud, and pretty much wired for jolly times when she mentioned over a period of several hours how she had: (a) climbed the Matterhorn Peak when she was an undergraduate student in Switzerland, (b) hunted the Great Horned Elk in Tibet during a holiday with her filthy rich friends from Dallas, and (c) water-skied in the show at Cyprus Gardens in Florida. Like a big dope, I gave her the Matterhorn and then the Great Horned Elk stories free and clear. However, I thought that the Cyprus Gardens waterskiing story was a bit much and I said so.

Unfortunately, that came out a lot too loud and too clear just when the rickety tic piano player took a potty break so everyone in the Rathskeller heard the end of my uncharacteristically uncomplimentary rant, especially to a good-looking, highly intelligent gal who had curves in places where most women don't even have places, and most especially a good-looking woman who bought her fair share of the beer and pretzels (i.e., that alone made her a "keeper."), was not your basic minimum daily requirement, and you surely wouldn't have to shake the sheets to find her.

Besides, all of my friends know that I am queer for good-looking girls.

Well, my stupid danged harangue right there in front of God and everybody went over like a turd in a punch bowl. So eee-mediately if not sooner, Rhea bailed out of our cozy booth in the back in the corner in the dark, and right away I knew that I had really screwed up what could have been a very good thing. Bummer! But my sudden brush with reality was too little and too late. Sadly, we never again held hands, played kneezies under the table, made "goo goo eyes" or whispered sweet somethings about an array of good things to come.

Back at the Sigma Chi house at an all-night fraternity/sorority block party, I learned from the resident All-American tailback that: (a) Rhea's stories were all true; (b) that Rhea had the Big Eye for tall, suntanned, unconditionally handsome, left-footed football kickers; and (c) that I had irrevocably blown my best chance for adventure galore in beautiful downtown Berkley at the University of California.

That's how I learned for sure that letting the cat out of the bag is a whole heck of a lot easier than putting the cat back in the bag. Do I hear another "Aaa-men!"?

22. LALA LAND

Many if not most of the student/hippies at the University of California at Berkley were intentionally rudderless, self-congratulatory, militantly anti-establishment, incredibly naive and uninformed for junior adults in any country, let alone downtown California. Initially, I stayed at the Sigma Chi fraternity house most weekends after playing inter-service football games. But later that year, I stopped by just to get away from the real world for a few hours in La La Land.

Since I was often short of civvies or I had just pulled MP duty, I often blended in by just taking off my tie and collar emblems, rolling up my uniform shirt sleeves so the stripes did not show, pulling down my trousers really low and slouching a bit. After a few months of those silly games, one evening I had to tell those hippies at the frat house and the Rathskeller Bar that I was being transferred to NAS Pensacola for flight training. Amazed, a whole bunch of them individually gave me the "peace" sign and said something like: "Wow man; I didn't know you are in the Marines."

Sometimes, it's the little things that mean a lot, even when their cornbread is not yet cooked in the middle.

23. JUDY'S SCHOOL SONG

Judy was a graduate music major at Berkley, and a darned good ricky tick, Gay 90s piano player who would occasionally sit in at the piano at the Rathskeller Bar for a couple of hours on Friday and/or Saturday nights. A plain looking, but pleasant older woman (i.e., older than 30), Judy loved to take requests in exchange for conversation and an occasional glass of white wine, which she could nurse longer than anyone except for a few on skid row.

Her claim to local fame was that she had never been stumped by a song request although many had tried but none could stump her. My impression was that Judy was loved by all, but dated by none. That's probably what happens in a raucous, free-wheeling basement bar like the Rathskeller when a gal wears her hair in a short Prince Valiant cut, granny glasses, mu mu dresses and comfortable low-heeled shoes.

Somehow, Bill Crowley became fixated about not being able to find a song that Judy could not play from memory. Each weekend that we were there, Bill would have three or four requests with which he thought he could finally stump her. However, just like clockwork, Judy would play each tune beautifully with absolutely no difficulty, and she often accompanied herself as she sang the whole song and all of the choruses just for the heck of it. Bill started off his challenges with something like "Down By The River In An Itty Bitty Brook" from the 1920s, and obscure old country/western forgettable tunes like "I Heard The Crash On The Highway, But I didn't Hear Anyone Pray" and "I Don't Care If It Snows Or Freezes As Long As I Have My Plastic Jesus, Standing

On The Dashboard Of My Car." Judy played them all, and I thought that she was terrific. But the whole challenge thing was bugging the heck out of Bill.

Finally, after about a month of Saturday nights, Bill was sure that he had found a song that Judy could not play. That night, he challenged her to play the school song of a particular high school in New York City which I guess that Bill had once attended. Laughing raucously, Judy yipped and then yelled "That's where I went to school" and played it all with bouncy gusto.

Talk about a coincidence. Whooohaa Nellie.

After that, we were happy to just gather around her piano to sing along or to listen when we could not hit the high notes. Bill and I never tried to stump Judy again. I always loved authentic Gay 90s ricky tick, honky tonk piano tunes, and I've never heard any that were played better than those that dear ol' Judy played and often sang with such great gusto. Bless her heart.

24. SIGGIES HANG TOGETHER

A young, very promising undergraduate Sigma Chi fraternity brother of Bill Crowley's was on the verge of dumping his pre-med career to marry a beautiful, local, bottle-blond floozy whose only apparent talents were well known to be between the sheets. Most of us didn't think that she had the brains that God gave a rubber duck, and many at the Rathskeller Bar were sure that she had been handled more than the ketchup bottle at the local truck stop. For that and a variety of other reasons that "till death do we part" arrangement was unacceptable to my pal Bill, several other Sigma Chi's at Berkley, and eventually me by association. Therefore, a drastic scheme was plotted over several pitchers of beer wherein one of Bill's Sigma Chi brothers would move in on the floozy (apparently not a real difficult trick), and the rest of us timed our evening to make sure that the love-sick undergrad would blunder into her apartment and catch them in their all-togethers.

To make a long story short, the timing was too darned good for a bunch of amateur plotters, the undergrad pre-med guy found his One

True Love jumping the other Siggies bones with gay abandon, and the wedding plans went down the dumper right then and there. Later, I heard that young Siggy found his way to John Hopkins and became a brain surgeon or something useful like that.

Don't you just love it when a plan comes together?

25. SAN JOSE NIGHTS

Late one night during the last hour of our 8 p.m. to midnight MP duty in San Jose, Joe D. and I were checking the local bars when we heard a loud racket in a booth in the back in a corner in the dark. Following the noise, Joe and I found a half-undressed, disheveled, drunken, trailer-trash honeychild screaming bloody murder while being man-handled by a gaggle of raucous drunken sailors while her soused sailor date held her firmly cheek-to-cheek in an arm lock and babbled to all about how much he loved her and only her, over and over again like a sodden mantra.

Grossly outnumbered by about a dozen to two, we put in a quick call for reinforcements. Then, considering the woman's immediate danger, we pulled out our night sticks, blew the heck out of our whistles, resurrected our old DI command presence voices, extracted her from those wild and crazy sailors, and took her outside after a tight-jawed confrontation with that drunken mob of hell-raisers. Actually, when on duty together, Joe and I never pulled out our .45-caliber pistols. Together, we did not need to do that.

After several attempts to calm her down in the fresh air, I tried unsuccessfully to get her name and address for our report before she would go home in a cab that we had hailed. But suddenly, just like flipping a toggle switch, she apparently had second thoughts, refused to be rescued, and went marching back to the mob of sailors still whooping it up and raising the roof in a back booth of that sleazy bar. Disgusted, Joe and I waved off the just arriving MP reinforcements and took the rest of the night off.

For me, that was a new high in lows. Joe D. seconded the motion.

26. PAY DAY PANIC

The night before payday, four of us grunts pooled the last of our money, bought a couple of jugs of local, cheap wine for about 79 cents each, and drank it in the barracks until we were all good and plenty snockered. The next morning before formal Guard Mount, I woke up with my mouth tasting like the bottom of a paul parrot cage. So I took a long drink of cold water and, unfortunately, the water mixed with the wine sediment still in the bottom of my stomach. Long story short, within minutes I was bombed out of my skull again, although I had formal Guard Mount duty as the U.S. flag bearer within the hour. Bad news. No one was available to take my place. Everybody had something else scheduled.

However, I was so afraid of the consequences of fouling up a USMC formal Guard Mount ceremony, and I was pumping so much adrenaline and focused like a laser that according to MSgt. O'Day, I performed that intricate, precise ceremony perfectly although I was fare-thee-well hammered during the entire ceremony. They tell me that faith can move mountains, but I am here to tell you that fear and adrenaline can really move this child even when all else fails.

27. PFC. GEORGE JONES' PICKING AND SINGING

I especially enjoyed singing country/western songs in the barracks with Pfc's George Jones, George Bailey, Bill Crowley and a few other Marines after a long day in the field. However, at that time, I thought that George Bailey was a better git-box picker and singer than future country/western Grammy winner and icon, George Jones. That shows you what kind of a tin ear I had.

With his smooth countrified baritone singing voice, George Jones had an amazing talent for pulling together and blending a bunch of untrained voices so that we actually sounded pretty darned good on occasion; at least we thought so. Additionally, he was the only person I even knew who could sing all 100 (or so) verses of that bawdy song: "The Man Who Comes To My House Every Single Day. *Pappa comes home and the man goes away...*" etc.

Although he did not drink adult beverages back in 1953, George Jones sang in various honkie tonks in the area even if he did not happen to have the formality of a valid gate pass that night. But that was no problem because darned near everybody in the barracks usually knew where George was performing on any given night, so if he was needed for some unscheduled duty, the Officer of the Day (OD) would send some of our MPs out to bring ol' George back to do his duty.

However, as MPs, we usually waited for an intermission so that George's mob of local fans would not take that excuse to riot and break stuff. Of course, when George saw our MPs coming in the front door, many times Ol' Possum would go an extra-long session without an intermission. I think that George Jones' theory at that time was "use it or lose it."

At that time, "Ghost Riders In The Sky" was a fairly popular song. In the privacy of our barracks, the veterans of the 5th Marine Brigade enjoyed occasionally converting the tune of "Ghost Riders" to the words of "The Marine Corps Hymn" and then adding a refrain to each of the three stanzas so that it went kind of like the following example. A clue: this works best when you first review the "Ghost Riders In The Sky" song in your mind a couple of times to get the feel and the phrasing of that particular song sorted out before starting with the Marine Corps Hymn. Here we go.

"From the Halls of Montezuma,
To the shores of Tripoleee (pause),
We will fight our country's battles,
In the air, on land and seeee (pause).
First to fight for right and freedom,
And to keep our honor cleannn (pause).
We are proud to claim the title of…
THE UNITED STATES MARINES.

(Refrain)
Gung Hoooo!
Semper Fiiii!
The United States Marines"

I figured that if anybody had the right to sing the "Marine Corps Hymn" to the tune of "Ghost Riders In The Sky," it was the veterans of the 5th Marine Brigade of the 1st Marine Division that mauled three ChiCom divisions while surrounded during the "Frozen Chosin Reservoir" campaign in the winter of 1950. These guys fought and won one of the greatest, most courageous battles in the history of warfare. I was honored to know them and serve with them. In combat, they were the best of the best. But around the barracks; sometimes not so much as you might think.

28. MOBILE MULTIPLE ROCKET LAUNCHERS

Early one evening, I was sitting alone while nursing a cold beer on a comfortable stool at the notorious Semper Fi Bar on the 13th floor of the Marine Memorial Hotel when a Marine Staff Sgt. wearing Korean War and WWII battle ribbons sat down at the last empty stool, which was between me and an old Gunny Sgt. who was also wearing Korean War and WWII ribbons. As they chatted over tall, cold, adult mixed drinks with dark Marine-green olives in them, the Gunny asked the SSgt. what unit he was with in Korea. The SSgt. said that he was a grunt mud Marine from the 1st Marine Regiment, 1st Battalion, Charlie Company serving with Col. (later Major General) Chesty Puller during the "Frozen Chosin" campaign.

Then the SSgt. asked the Gunny what unit he was with in Korea. The Gunny said that he had been with a mobile multiple launch rocket unit for artillery fire support at the division level. The Gunny had no sooner said that when the SSgt. knocked his superior noncommissioned officer right off his stool and onto the floor, where the Gunny lingered a few seconds as he apparently pondered what the heck he had said to make the SSgt so darned mad that he would knock a higher ranking NCO to the floor, especially out in public. That's a punishable "No No" that will remove hard-earned stripes very quickly in my U.S. Marine Corps.

Right away, the SSgt. helped the Gunny to his feet and explained apologetically that his sudden, seemingly irrational conduct was nothing personal, but was more of a reflex left over from Korea. He went on to describe how he and his unit were comfortably dug in across from an entire Chinese division that did not want to mess around with a reinforced Marine regiment, especially when the North Koreans were about finished with fussing over the shape of the conference table for the cease fire negotiations with the UN command.

At that time, the shooting war had essentially ground down to a political peeing contest along the 38th parallel, and nobody on either side of the DMZ wanted to be the last Marine or the last ChiCom dirt farmer killed before a long-overdue cease fire would become a historic Kodak moment.

According to the SSgt., a 4-by-4 truck pulled an 18-rocket launcher (I thought it was 18 rockets per load, but now I'm not so sure) that pulled up just behind his bunker on the Marine MLR, setup quickly, then fired all the rockets in a single ripple. As the last rocket left its tube, the 4-by-4 truck driver eee-mediately popped the clutch on the truck and the empty launcher and crew were off like a bat out of hell in a cloud of dust just before the ChiCom 152 mm artillery began a pounding counter-battery barrage that broke things and hurt Marines for the remainder of the day. That was when that SSgt. vowed to deck the first mobile rocket artilleryman he met, no matter who and no matter when.

Unfortunately the Gunny had the untimely bad karma to be the first one the SSgt. met after returning from Korea. It was nothing personal, and in the light of that sea story, the Gunny said that he fully understood and took no offense.

When I got up to meet Pfc. Bill Crowley and head for the Rathskeller Bar in Berkley, the Gunny and the SSgt. were still sitting at the bar swilling tall, cold, adult mixed drinks, paying in rotation, and telling their individual sea stories about Iwo Jima, Okinawa, Pusan and the frozen Chosin campaign. If either of those two old salts ever say that the berries are ripe, you had better get your bucket. You can bet your bippy that they KNOW what's what in my Marine Corps.

29. BOUNCY BALL HOOK SHOTS

Basketball was not my game, but I had played second-string in both high school and junior college just to fill out the squad for practice scrimmages, and to keep in shape between football and baseball seasons. So when football season was over at NAS Moffett Field, I tried out for the base basketball team and to my great surprise, I made the first-string varsity team as a starter. I guess that I had gotten better after missing the previous season when my hands were broken, but my juco team won the national juco basketball championship without me. It occurred to me that maybe my leaving made the El Dorado Grizzlies basketball squad a somewhat better team.

Most Armed Forces bouncy ball teams were vertically challenged back then because you would not find too many seven footers in the enlisted ranks to play center. In fact, the tallest guy on the Moffett Red Raiders was a 6-foot 5-inch sailor who played forward. Pfc. Joe Bolling and I were both 6-foot 3-inch forwards because we were sure as heck neither guards nor centers. Service teams usually have a lot of relatively short, quick guards. We had more than our fair share, but big holes everywhere else.

So the schedule was set and we had to play with what we had. Without a big center, we often used three guards to move the ball down the court and the two forwards to crisscross back and forth across the free-throw paint to take whatever shots we could get by checking the other team's center when our other forward had the ball. Our big guy had a pretty good jump shot so we forwards took turns relieving whoever was tired.

About all I had was a soft left-handed floater of a hook shot that I would bank off the backboard from directly in front of the goal as I passed by from right to left. Improbable as it may be, we won some games that way against some taller teams who should have won if "tall" was the only metric. Before that, I kind of thought that it was.

I remember one home game against a Navy base team when I scored 18 points with my soft, left-handed hook shot. I didn't score any free throws that night, probably because they would not let me shoot free throws with a hook shot (at least that's my story and I am going to stick with it). After the game, both teams were having a late supper together when the other team's center wandered over to where I was eating and asked me in all seriousness: "Dave, are you left handed?" I told him "Heck no. I was just spotting you guys that much."

30. "OH YES YOU WILL"

One afternoon, the fire alarm went off in the Marine barracks and interrupted several payday poker games scattered around the barracks. Already in our dungarees, about a dozen of us in the area dropped everything, grabbed our rifles, helmets and 782 web gear, and ran to the Corporal of the Guard post in the basement near the brig. There we learned that the fire was burning out of control on both the 1st and 2nd decks at the other end of the same red brick, U-shaped building where we were billeted.

So we took a shortcut through the building and got to the fire way ahead of the Navy Crash Crews/Firemen who had been working at the other end of our 2 ½ mile long duty runway and were just starting on their way back. I believe that we could hear them coming, but they still had a long way to go.

As the other Marines spread out to handle security and crowd control, the Officer of the Day (OD), MSgt. O'Day, sent me and another Marine into the burning building to make sure that everyone had been evacuated. I took the second deck and my buddy took the first deck.

"Have no fear, the Marines are here."

The fire on the second floor was a roaring, blazing inferno with heavy black smoke in the barracks area of the Navy Casual Company, so there was not much I could do there except yell a lot and stay low. However, I heard no response and that area was getting awfully unlivable with unknown things popping, sizzling and exploding all over the place so I moved on ahead of the expanding blaze. Anything in that fire was toast.

As I was kind of duck waking low to stay under the swirling black, choking smoke, I heard a couple of guys singing loud and proud in the showers as if nothing was wrong. Apparently those guys were using very hot water so that the effects of the turbulent steam in there were still strong enough to somewhat block the smoke from burbling into their shower area.

All hell was breaking loose outside of the shower room, but those two sailors did not have a clue that the building was burning down around them. They were singing so loud and were covered with soap and shampoo when I got right up to them in their showers before they knew that I was in the room with them.

Obviously, we had to get the heck out of there darned quick or we would be cut off at the one door exit. However, there was another problem. Get this; we were squatting down in the hall to stay below the thick black smoke, and the roar of the fire and things breaking and exploding in the heat were getting too darned close for comfort. However, both of those guys wanted to go back to their blazing quarters to get their clothes.

I could not believe it, so I had to get in their faces and use my old DI voice and vocabulary to convince them that everything back there was burning like the four corners of hell, and if we did not get the heck out of there very quickly, we would be burning too. That was not an exaggeration. I could not understand why they could not understand the danger we were in at that time.

All these two sailors had to wear were two fairly small, government issued towels, flip flop sandals, and nothing else. Then, when they looked out a second-story window at the gathering crowd below, many of whom were Waves, both sailors stubbornly insisted that they were not going to go out there like that, as if they had any other choice. They did not, so I put my bayonet on the business end of my M1 rifle and assured them that yeah, we would do that very thing, and we would do it eee-mediately if not sooner. I was not about to fry just because they were about to die.

So I herded those two very reluctant sailors down the stairs under protest. We stopped at the outside door where both of them looked out and repeated that they were not going out there as the fast-moving fire seemed to half way surround us. That's when I reverted to Marine Drill

Instructor one more time and literally muscled them out the door with my rifle just before the base firemen came running in with their hoses and knocking down everything that was not a permanent structure. I had to jump back to avoid getting a fire hose stuffed in my face.

I was putting my bayonet back in my scabbard when our C.O., a full bull colonel and another veteran of the 5th Marine Brigade, walked up, shook my hand and assured me that I had just earned a Navy/Marine Letter of Commendation. For crap sakes, minus the Combat "V," that's what my blood brother "Permanent Pfc." Eladio Gonzales earned for saving the lives of his recon patrol during a deadly fire fight with the bad guys in Korea. That's just pure crazy. Hell's bells, all I expected was an "Atta' Boy" and a couple of cold beers from those two sailors at the enlisted slop chute some night around payday.

31. IT'S ALWAYS SOMETHING

Of all of the grunt Marine enlisted men who passed all of the qualification tests and were initially appointed to go to OCS at Quantico, Virginia, not one in our original group of a dozen would ever get to OCS. Of all of the guys I knew who were initially qualified to go to Quantico, all but one would have been great Mustang officers (promoted from the enlisted ranks) in my estimation. Like my Uncle Charley Dunn often said: "There is many a slip between the cup and the lip." Uncle Charley was a very wise old guy.

Anxious to jumpstart the stalled process while I was at NAS Moffett Field, I volunteered for duty as a working DI for the OCS classes at Quantico until my number would finally come up. Then I figured that I could just change hats and take the same course as an officer candidate. That would have been an obvious cake walk, and I was certainly ready for that transition eee-mediately if not sooner.

Unfortunately, that idea was unprecedented, and it subsequently fell by the way side although I am pretty sure that the colonel, my Commanding Officer, went for it and gave me a recommendation to do just that. I understand that someone near the top of the Marine food chain of command had believed that the concept of sending highly qualified grunts to OCS had merit. However, someone else, probably an elitist "ring knocker" with more rank than my Commanding Officer, was either a better politician or more determined, so that the program was set back and back and back until all of the original candidates were assigned to other Marine Occupational Specialties (MOSs) after wasting their time waiting until they were half way through their initial enlistment.

Like Anna Roseanna Roseannadanna often said: "It's always something."

32. SSGT REYES' BOXING LESSON

The first time I met Staff Sgt. Reyes, a bunch of us lower-ranking enlisted troops had fallen out for some kind of an exercise on the drill field. SSgt. Reyes was a fairly sturdy and tough-minded NCO who had a darned good record on the WWII and Korean battlefields and was, I believe, mentioned in the book *"The New Breed."* The first thing that he said to our assembled group of mostly Korean veterans was that we would do exactly what he told us to do, when he told us to do it, because not only was he a Staff Sgt. (and we were not), but also because he would kick our butts if we did not get with the program eee-mediately if not sooner.

Somehow, I did not believe that butt kicking routine, so I told him with all due respect that of course I would obey his commands because he was a SSgt. and I was not. However, I did not believe that he could kick my butt.

A firecracker with a short fuze, SSgt. Reyes immediately challenged me to get in the boxing ring at the gym with him, so I did. Just before the first round of a standard two minute, three-round match, I told him that he really did not want to get in that ring with me, and he darned sure did not want to box with me either. He disagreed, the bell rang, and SSgt. Reyes went down for the count in the first 30 seconds of the first round. That was enough. He hadn't laid a glove on me, and I had used him for a punching bag. SSgt. Reyes didn't need any more convincing. He just needed to make a few changes in his oral command presence and his situational awareness.

Hells bells, I must have outweighed him by 30 pounds and was in good shape. He may have been a decent bar room brawler in his day, but I had been a bar room bouncer who earned my pay check by tossing trouble makers and brawlers like him out of Jerry Leonard's Club in El Dorado, Kansas as quickly and quietly as possible.

A couple of nights later in a bar near the base, SSgt. Reyes had been drinking way too much again when I first noticed him at the other end of the bar. Eventually, somebody, a civilian I think, yelled that a whole bunch of sailors were next door at a honkie tonk, and they were looking for some Marines. Immediately, SSgt. Reyes climbed down off his bar stool and headed out the door with a half-finished long-neck beer bottle in his hand.

Anybody could see that he was in no condition for a brawl or anything else not related to soaking up adult beverages, so I went after him right after I finished my beer. Unfortunately, I did not catch up with him until just after he staggered to the middle of the dance floor and yelled: "Any of you damned swabbies looking for a Marine? Well, here I am you @#$%&+%$#s. You want a piece of me? Come and get it."

In a flash, Reyes and I were surrounded by a solid wall of irate and thoroughly sloshed sailors that encircled us on a radius of less than four feet, and those sailors were at least three deep all around that circle. Any fool could see that there was no way out, and I figured that this was going to hurt a lot. However, before a single punch could be thrown, the Navy Shore Patrol (SP) guys arrived and blew their whistles a lot. Instantly, that huge herd of sailors disappeared like wind-blown smoke, leaving SSgt. Reyes and me as the only people standing on the whole danged dance floor.

So the SPs did their job, escorted us into the back of their caged paddy wagon, and hauled us away. However, a few blocks away from the ruckus, the SP paddy wagon pulled over to the curb, and the old Chief Petty Officer in charge turned us loose again with the warning not to go back to that bar again that night, and be sure to not get into a one-sided ruckus like that again. After handshakes all around, SSgt. Reyes staggered into another bar, and I went back to the barracks to get some sleep. I had enjoyed all of the fun that I could handle for one evening.

The next morning in the chow hall, I ran into the same SP Chief and thanked him for the professional courtesy he had given me and SSgt. Reyes the preceding night. Naturally, I allowed as how I owed him a favor, not knowing what was going to happen a few nights later. The Chief and I were both off duty that morning, so we sat near an active coffee pot, scrounged a few more sugar doughnuts, and got acquainted.

The Chief had been in the Navy since 1924, and had grown up in Newton Station, Kansas, not 20 miles north of my hometown of Wichita. Since we both came from the flatlander world, we Jayhawks usually hang together so we won't be hung individually. That works for me, anyway.

33. CPL. "FRENCHY" BESSIER

Corporal "Frenchy" Bessier was a tall, dark and handsome young Marine veteran of the Korean War. When I knew him, he could have been the stuff of a Marine recruit poster except for the fact that he was also certifiably nuts. However, he came by it honestly.

Earlier in Korea, Cpl. Bessier was captured by the newly arrived Chinese Army when his heavy duty, reinforced bunker was hit by a Chinese 152 mm high explosive artillery shell that caved it in on him so he could not move. Barely conscious and wounded, Bessier was overrun by a horde of grunt Chinese infantry who eventually dug him out of the rubble, treated his wounds, stole his wrist watch and wallet, and tossed him into a Chinese prison camp somewhere around the Yalu River on the Chinese border with northern North Korea.

After a couple of months of standing around looking at oriental desolation through a barbed wire fence, eating fish heads and a small ball of putrid rice every day, Cpl. Bessier got tired of the boring routine of prison life, so he went under the wire and over the hill, and headed south toward the Marine lines along the "De-Militarized Zone" (DMZ) at the 38th parallel that was a darned long way to the south. Hiding by day and moving ever southward at night, he played serious hide-and-seek games in a heavily militarized sector for something like a month or more before almost being shot by his buddies when he came back through the wire at the Marine Main Line of Resistance (MLR) looking a lot more like a Chinese scare crow than a U.S. Marine reporting for duty.

That must have been quite an amazing journey because Bessier is a little over six feet tall, and the local farm peons and even the military troops along his route were mostly five feet and a couple inches tall to five feet and eight inches tall so there was no way that he could blend into a crowd or a chow line, especially in his tattered Chinese prison/Marine dungaree clothes. But somehow, he fast-fingered enough edibles to keep moving south and to avoid the seemingly never ending gaggles of Chinese and goose-stepping Korean soldiers also headed south.

After a lot of medical, mental and dental rehabilitation at Oak Knoll Hospital in San Francisco, Cpl. Bessier was stationed at NAS Moffett Field to wait for his normal discharge date. Cleared for only the lightest of light duty, eventually this led to that, and that led to the other, and before we knew it, Cpl. Bessier and I were assigned to the Main Gate on the 8 p.m. to midnight watch, and sometimes to the midnight to 4 a.m. "graveyard" watch. When you talk about a setup for the perfect storm, that was it.

About a week or so after that Shore Patrol Chief Petty Officer saved my bacon in the SSgt. Reyes fiasco, Cpl. Bessier and I were standing tall at the Main Gate at about 1 a.m. in the morning when we heard a police siren in the distance that seemed to be coming our way fairly fast. Pretty soon, we saw the SP Chief's old 1939 Chevy four-door jalopy rounding the big sweeping right-hand curve in the road to the Main Gate. Obviously, the Mountain View cops were chasing him, but had not yet come into our view. I yelled to Bessier: "He's that SP Chief I told you about. I owe him a favor. Let him in." We both jumped out of the way and waved him on as the Chief drove through that full stop gate and then 10 mph speed-limit base road at about 70 mph with his foot in the carburetor and the hammer down. He was definitely moving on.

Immediately after the Chief disappeared into the first side street off the base's main boulevard, a Mountain View Police car came around that sweeping right-hand curve in a four-wheel drift, down shifted and then accelerated toward our gate like a charging bull.

NOTE: Do NOT ever try to run through a Marine gate without Marine permission unless you have a death wish. We could see that those cops thought that they could do an encore following the Chief's lead because the Chief obviously had not stopped. That encore was not going to happen.

Both Cpl. Bessier and I pulled out our Colt M1911 .45-caliber pistols, jacked rounds into both of our firing chambers, and we stood in the middle of the entry side of the gate side by side with our pistols aimed directly at the oncoming cop car. Both of us were prepared to shoot out that cop's radiator if he did not stop. Thank goodness, the driver got the message and used the last 180 feet or so and probably his hand brake as well to come to a screeching halt right in front of the main gate. Boy, was I relieved. I had never shot at a cop before, but there could be a first time for everything if they thought that they would run through that Marine gate without stopping.

As I continued to stand directly in front of the police car with my raised .45 in my left hand at something like parade rest, Cpl. Bessier slowly walked over to the driver's side of the car and cheerfully but politely greeted the driver. "Good morning sir," he said. "Welcome to NAS Moffett Field. May I assist you, sir?"

Mad as a wet hen/er'cop, the driver yelled: "You're damned right you can. We are in hot pursuit of that g'damned old Chevy that just went through this g'damned gate." Bessier looked intently at the black and white police cruiser with flashing red gum ball light on top, large Mountain View Police emblem on the car door, both cops in full police uniforms with badges and patches and duty belts and all of that good cop stuff, and then he said: "Yes sir. But first, do you have any identification, sir?" The cop grumbled something unintelligible, jerked his billfold out of his hip pocket and held it out the window for Cpl. Bessier to read.

Low key, polite to a fault, Bessier asked the cop to please remove his drivers' ID from his billfold and then hand that ID to Bessier. The cop did what he was asked to do and handed his drivers' ID to Bessier, which Bessier studied intently as if he had never seen such an ID before. Finally, after a long pause, Bessier said to the cop: "Do you still live at (blank blank) Maple Street, sir?" The cop said that he did, so Bessier returned the ID to the cop and nodded for me to put my .45 pistol back in my holster.

As the cop put his stick shift into low gear, Bessier pointed at the other cop and said: "Who is your passenger, Officer (whoever)?" By that time, the cop in the passenger seat was holding his ID up in his billfold for Bessier to see through the front windshield. As if deep in thought, Bessier walked slowly around the front of the cop car and then proceeded to go through the exact same rain dance with the police officer in the passenger seat. After about as long a time as that process could be stretched out, Bessier was finally satisfied that those two men in police uniforms and an obvious police car really were policemen.

Then, just for grins, Bessier took one last stalling ploy. He walked over to the gate shack, picked up the watch log, and asked the driver: "Excuse me sir. What is the purpose of your visit again?" The driver answered: "We were in hot pursuit of a drunk damned driver who went through this damned gate a few minutes ago" Bessier carefully wrote that down, repeated the cop's statement, and then nodded to me again. I stepped out of the street so that the police cruiser could continue in hot pursuit at the posted 10 miles an hour speed limit while two stony faced Marines saluted their visitors in unison.

I could not have done it better myself.

About an hour later, the two police officers returned to the little town of Mountain View, California, through the exit lane of the main gate as Bessier and I rendered hand salutes and invited them to stop by our Naval Air Station at any time. We assured them that Mountain View police officers are always welcome.

Just before lunch the next morning, I bumped into the SP Chief again in the chow hall. He said that he had hid his old and very distinctive 1939 four-door Chevy inside the huge blimp hangar, and then the night crew of that FASRON support service squadron shut the giant clamshell doors tightly so that no one could see inside or come inside the hangar without the total cooperation of the Navy motorized door operators inside the blimp hangar. Those doors are so huge that each one is mounted on several railroad flatbed cars that move on standard railroad tracks.

Over a couple of cups of coffee with sugar doughnuts to match, we both agreed that the Chief and I were pretty much even as far as favors were concerned.

Go Navy. Semper fi, y'all.

34. THE INFAMOUS PROPELLER CLUB

After a one-car rollover wreck with six Marines and one tipsy Wave aboard near the El Camino Real highway between Mountain View and NAS Moffett Field, Cpl. Tillery and I crawled out of the broken side windows, finally popped one of the jammed doors open, and pulled the rest of the injured out of what was left of the upside down 1947 Mercury Club Coupe. Then we rendered first aid to the best of our abilities (I was a certified first aid instructor at that time), made the other five victims as comfortable as possible because they weren't going to go anywhere under their own power very soon, and then we hit the ditches and went into an evasive mode when the oncoming police car and ambulance were only several blocks away.

We were sure that we had better reduce the number of occupants down to five because the police would surely raise all kinds of hell about seven people being crammed into a small car driven by whichever Marine would prove to be less hammered when the cops arrived. I believed that at least one of our Marines was actually pretty sober, so they should have done all right. Besides, we knew that whoever would finally be declared the driver had only swerved to cause the rollover on that two-lane blacktop road to miss a cute little mama bunny rabbit and her brood of very cute little baby bun rabbits that were crossing the road. That was their story such as it was, so they knew that they had better stick with it come hell or high water.

After we had walked to within a couple of blocks outside the main gate to Moffett Field, Cpl. Tillery decided that he was going to make a pit stop at a really tough hillbilly bar, The Propeller Club, which I had only visited as an MP on patrol with Pfc. Joe D. (Jody) Bolling riding shotgun. We were both 6 feet and 3 inches tall, about 215 pounds, and when on duty in some bad-assed honkie tonk, most drunks and tough guys usually disappeared when we came through the front door. Overall, we tended to look like we wished that somebody/anybody would do us a favor and start something. That impression does tend to dampen the usual fun and games at such places until after Jody and I had checked for drunk military personnel needing a ride back to their base, and then we boogied on down the road.

However, on that particular night, I was hurting from a smashed foot (it had fallen out of the back seat side window and the roof of the car had rolled over on it several times) that would put me on light duty as turnkey in our brig for about a month. So I hobbled over to the base sickbay and gave them the usual "I dropped my locker box on my foot" story which nobody believes but every Marine uses when he does not feel like sharing any more information than necessary with someone who he feels does not need to know any of these pertinent details anyway.

The next morning, I met Cpl. Tillery in the chow hall. He was wearing another white head wrap somewhat like that swami head bandage he had worn when he came back from Oklahoma. I asked him if that Propeller Club bar was as tough as I had heard. Since I asked, he told me how he had sat on a stool at the bar with a big bloody flap of scalp hanging down over his ear like a large inverted "V" oozing blood on a bar rag as he downed a couple of stiff mixed drinks. However, nobody in that bar said one darned thing to him about his obvious injury, as if that was such a common occurrence that it was not worth mentioning.

That did it. There was no doubt in my mind. That Propeller Club was certifiably a very rough, tough, bad-assed bar, which I avoided except when on duty as an armed MP motor patrol cop. Then, I always walked into that bar like I owned the place.

35. ENGLISH GRAMMAR CLASSES

You may have guessed by now that I was very pleased—make that "honored"—to serve with the heroic Marine warriors of the 5th Marine Regiment of the 1st Marine Division who fought and won the moving series of battles against three ChiCom divisions that had encircled them during the "Frozen Chosin Reservoir" campaign. Their initially defensive fight turned offensive battle in the snow-covered mountains under blizzard conditions rates right up there with such iconic battles as the 300 Spartans at the battle of Thermopylae in 480 B.C. who held off at least 150,000 Persians (some Greek historians counted a million Persians) at a chokepoint until the Greeks could assemble their forces to destroy the Persian fleet and win the war. About 2,430 years later, the 1st Marine Division decimated the three ChiCom divisions that had been assigned to destroy the 1st Marines, and brought out all of their dead and wounded as well as many U.S. Army stragglers and wounded U.S. Army soldiers abandoned in U.S. Army field hospitals.

Many of these proven warriors could cope with, and prevail in most grunt Marine activities with the exception of writing letters back home to parents, wives, girl-friends, siblings and such. In that one regard, many of our Marines were not so good, so when asked, I helped a number of these fine warriors by occasionally editing and otherwise improving the English grammar in their personal letters.

Over time, I became something like their unofficial English tutor, then progressed to occasional chalk talks to explain nouns, verbs, adjectives, adverbs, etc., and even taught them the basics of diagramming simple sentences so that they could have a better command of the written English language. These guys were not stupid or bad students. They were eager to learn, but apparently they were unfortunate to have had really lousy English teachers in high school. That was not their fault and I felt sorry for them.

I remember that my first classroom session was about 60 minutes long and covered only nouns and verbs. By keeping it simple, my students made terrific progress with a formerly mind-boggling bugaboo. We started with something like: "A noun is a person, place or thing. For example: LtCol. Ray Murray (a person), his rifle (a good thing), and Korea (a lousy place to live or die). Am I going too fast for you?" We played with that concept until everybody was onboard and comfortable with the initial concept. Then we took a piss call, I offered one of my mom's then-famous divinity cookies to each student, poured some more coffee, and moved on to tackle the verbs.

I then explained that verbs are action words that state that something is happening, has happened, will happen or could happen. They learned that verbs are used in: (1) making a statement like "Col. Chesty Puller led the 1st Marines," (2) asking a question like "Who took my damned pogy bait?", and (3) giving a command like "You will run around the blimp hangar twice." We played around with those two concepts together, had quite a bit of class participation, and called it a day.

In the next class, we worked on subjects and sentences; i.e., "a sentence is a group of words that contains a subject and a verb, and is a complete thought." The biggest stumbling block for many of our guys was sorted out by: "without a verb, any group of words is only a feeble fragment and not a complete sentence." Funny thing; I always left my chalk talk on the blackboard after class and surprise, surprise, those notes stayed there for quite a bit longer than I would have thought. One time, my notes stayed on the blackboard a whole week until our next class, although these classrooms were in constant use.

With God's help and a long handled swagger stick-like pointer, we made significant progress in each succeeding class. I was more than glad to help those guys. Just like any other discipline, we defined the major elements, got comfortable with them, worked into the gnarly specifics in easy stages, and then each one went for his own personal best qualification. However, nobody flunked in my classes.

Like that wise old former rodeo cowboy back in El Dorado, Kansas often reminded me: "When eating an elephant, take just one bite at a time."

As you were.

36. ACCIDENTAL DISCHARGE

As I returned from escorting a general court-marshal prisoner from pre-dawn breakfast with a loaded .45 pistol on my hip, my buddy Pfc. Joe D. Bolling (later Lt.Col. Bolling) arrived exactly on schedule to relieve me. Since Joe was always late (every single time, without exception until that morning), I was so surprised that when I removed the ammo magazine from my .45 pistol during the weapon exchange with Joe, somehow I did not look closely enough through the receiver into the firing chamber.

Like I said, I was really incredibly startled when Joe showed up on time for the first time. When I pointed the weapon at the wall to dry fire it, the .45 discharged, the bullet ricocheted off two steel walls and came back over my shoulder, and the tough-guy general court-marshal prisoner standing near me dropped to his knees, hugging his gut, and began puking his just-eaten breakfast all over the deck. Additionally, it did not help that my left hand was bleeding ("Sir, I dropped a locker box on my hand").

Shocked, I looked at the doubled-over prisoner who I thought could have been wounded too, then down the hall at the wide-eyed Cpl. of the Guard and the startled Motor Patrol Sgt. who was standing beside him. I've got to admit that for a nanosecond I thought about shooting my way out of that building full of some of the finest Marine warriors of all times. That was not a good idea.

Laconically, Joe lightened the tense moment by saying: "Wow! Now what the heck are you going to do for an encore, Dave?" Long story short, possibly because I was on the elite 12 enlisted pilot training fast track that iconic Colonel Chesty Puller had initiated, our combat weary Commanding Officer did not nail me to a cross, but only gave me a month of an hour or two of extra duty each weekday evening in his office shuffling paper, probably because there were darned few in that whole detachment who could type. Our only office pinky did not type worth a flip and needed all of the help that he could get. Heck, I was more than glad to help out.

Thank goodness that faux pas was never entered in my record; possibly because our C.O.'s 5th Marine veterans of the house-to-house battles in Seoul and the iconic battles at frozen Chosin were constantly using up much of their issued ammo by shooting at sea gulls during their reclusive guard watches on our dock on San Francisco Bay. Remember that some of those guys had been on line fighting the North Koreans and ChiComs darned near every day for well over a year. The colonel seemed to take a relaxed approach for his battle weary Marines, and I guess that some of that slopped over on me.

Gung ho. Semper fi.

37. "HALT OR I WILL SHOOT YOU!"

One evening just after supper, a previously easy going potential general court-marshal prisoner casually mentioned to me through the bars that he was going to escape the next morning during the usual march to pre-dawn breakfast before everyone else on the base could eat their breakfasts. Right away, I thought that he was kidding me, or maybe just playing mind games with me. So I told him that wasn't a good idea because he could get shot that way; by me, if necessary, although I'd really hate to do that. However, he doggedly repeated his threat to escape the next morning. I guess that he had it all figured out and had to tell somebody, but telling the brig turnkey certainly wasn't the place to start.

Since our usual banter through the bars had turned into a threat to escape; that was a serious situation, and I knew that I needed some fanny coverage sooner rather than later. So I called the Officer of the Day, a "mustang" Marine Captain (i.e., he was promoted from the enlisted ranks) who told both the prisoner and me in no uncertain terms that if the prisoner tried to escape, I was ordered to shoot him.

Furthermore, the Captain also warned me that if the prisoner did get away, I would take the prisoner's place until he was recaptured. I responded: "Aye aye, Sir" which in Navy/Marine terms means "I hear you and I will obey you." I had my necessary fanny coverage because I was pretty darned sure that prisoner was not blowing smoke, and I did not want a big ration of crap after I would have to shoot him with my Colt .45-caliber side arm. That big bore weapon would ruin that prisoner's day, week, month, year or life no matter where it would hit him.

The next morning—such a coincidence—darned if the base Motor Patrol truck was temporarily out of service for some darned reason, and time was running out until everybody else on the base would fill up the chow hall to have breakfast. That was a major No No. Prisoners cannot mix with non-prisoners in the chow hall, especially a potential general court-marshal prisoner. Ergo, without the necessary Motor Patrol backup, which was supposed to follow me with two Marines and at least one shotgun, I had to escort four prisoners along the poorly lit, pre-dawn streets to the chow hall.

Our Commanding Officer, that full-bull colonel and veteran of the "Frozen Chosin Reservoir" battles expected his Marines to make decisions on their feet and execute them responsibly. It was my call and I took it. So I jacked a round into my .45 pistol's firing chamber to save me a second or two if needed, put it back in my holster, and we were off to the chow hall without the Motor Patrol truck trailing behind our little formation.

After marching several hundred yards down the still fairly dark road, suddenly, as advertised, that potential general court-marshal prisoner broke ranks and ran down a side street directly under a bright street light. I shouted to him to halt as I pulled out my .45 caliber pistol. That young sailor was surprisingly fast, and if I had said "Halt" three times according to Standard Operating Procedures (SOPs), he would have been around the corner and out of sight. If I had chased that young fellow, the other three prisoners probably would not be there when I returned, and then I would have been in a mell of a hess.

As I was aiming my .45 with a perfect sight picture of my target under the street light, breathing in and letting out half of that breath while squeezing the trigger, the tardy motor patrol truck raced around me and one of the MPs yelled: "Hey Dave, don't shoot. We got 'em." Thank goodness. They finally recaptured the prisoner when he got tired of trying to outrun our pick'em-up truck and shotgun toting MPs.

I am a bit embarrassed to admit that while I was in the process of probably making a big, usually fatal hole in that young sailor, my mind was racing as I was thinking that the investigating court would automatically fine me the usual $2 and transfer me to another Navy/Marine base of my choice. As I was breathing and squeezing the .45's trigger with that perfect, well-lit sight picture at only about 50 feet or so downrange, in my mind I was trying to decide whether I would prefer to be transferred to Hawaii or Japan. Mea culpa, mea culpa, mea maxima culpa.

Where I come from, first we do something and then we talk about it.

38. PURPLE HEART

Early one morning before reveille, I was still half asleep while shaving in the head (i.e., bathroom). Drowsy as the dickens, I asked a young Hispanic Marine who was shaving next to me about where he had been wounded since he had received the Purple Heart in Korea. Since he had been wounded by a shrapnel grenade that exploded very close behind him, he said that he had been wounded "all over." Not yet fully awake, I continued shaving as I mumbled: "Yeah. That's a bad place." Minutes later, I could not believe that I had actually made that idiotic remark.

39. "AAA-GILE, MO-BILE AND HOS-TILE"

A middleweight at best, my good buddy Pfc. Bill Crowley challenged me, a former honkie-tonk nightclub bouncer and an experienced heavyweight boxer with a bunch of wins in the boxing ring and no losses anywhere else either. Naturally, I thought that with the weight and size disparity, ol' Bill must be a very tough, very good boxer to demand to take me on. Since I did not want to get a big surprise and possibly a sore jaw again like when I was doping off in the ring with a good friend back home who was "deaf and dumb," but a professional boxer who did a quick number on my face before I could figure him out.

Anyway, bottom line, I protected myself by hitting Bill with everything but the ring posts right after the first bell. Sadly, I broke his nose several seconds later at about the same instant that I realized that Bill was not much of a boxer at all. Curiously, he just wanted to see what it was like to be in a boxing ring.

Feeling awful about what had just happened, I took Bill to the base sickbay where a Navy Corpsman asked him who had broken his nose so badly. Still pumped up and feisty, Crowley jumped to his feet, mad as the dickens and faced down the sailor growling: "It wasn't no danged swabbie!" Of course, the incident was reported as another dropped locker box. Bill knew the drill.

Crowley then decided that his problem was that he just wasn't big enough to whip my donkey, so he began a concentrated weight-lifting program and an eating regimen that did him a world of good. I believe that he had a boxing tutor as well. Anyway, as he grew bigger and stronger, he continually reminded me, usually in a very casual, friendly manner that: "One of these days when I get just a little bigger, I'm going to break your nose, Dave."

Fortunately, I was transferred to NAS Pensacola a couple of months later because my buddy Bill was turning into a very large, muscular, and potentially menacing guy. All of that good food in such large quantities at NAS Moffett Field—"the best chow in the U.S. Navy"—was the perfect training table for a highly motivated guy like Bill had become. Knowing Bill for so long, I was sure that he would eventually demand a second bout just as a personal goal to aim for.

At some other military bases, the food in the chow halls could have been graded as cruel and unusual nourishment.

40. MARINE CORPS BIRTHDAY BASH

On 10 November 1953, the USMC birthday, U.S. Navy Shore Patrol personnel temporarily took over almost all security duties at NAS Moffett Field so that almost all Marines could have the honor of attending the Marine Corps Birthday party at the on-base Marine Headquarters building. I said "almost all Marines" because protocol dictated that at least one motor patrol vehicle must be manned by Marines at all times with no exceptions. Out of at least 100 Marine candidates, Pfc. Eladio Gonzales and I drew the short straws, so we had the duty during the duration of the formal birthday celebration.

Of course, we did stop by Headquarters for a piece of the USMC birthday cake, but we could not take the time to feast on turkey with all of the trimmings, and we definitely could not drink beer from any of the half dozen free kegs while we were on duty. However, we could stop by occasionally on our rounds, smell all of the good stuff cooking in the kitchen while the birthday speeches were given, and watch many of our buddies swilling the suds while we could do nothing but standby to standby.

After about the third round of our window peeking at the party (like waifs with noses plastered against the glass window at a candy store), our "can do" reflexes took over. Eladio reached through the open kitchen window and picked up an entire baked turkey on a pan while I light fingered a pitcher of beer off a handy serving tray while the servers were looking the other direction. Fully provisioned, we drove a couple of miles over to the rows of massive concrete ammunition bunkers at the base ammunition depot. There, under a bright but not full moon, Eladio and I ate as much of that big ol' turkey and stuffing as we could at that time, and washed it down with the pitcher of Budweiser or whatever that belly wash was.

After another armed patrol pass around that huge base, still gnawing on the turkey carcass sitting on the bench seat between us, we were finally relieved at midnight when the normal Marine MP chores were reinstated. So we parked the pick'em-up truck and took what was left of the turkey into the Marine barracks while still stuffing our faces and looking for a convenient place to stow the evidence of the crime.

Very tired, over stuffed and pretty well stumble prone, we finally disposed of the stripped, still pretty much-stuffed turkey carcass between the sheets at the foot of the still-empty rack of a 17-year young Marine who was awaiting his 18th birthday so that he could transfer to "FMF Mud Marine" duty in Korea. Our mission accomplished, we both hit the sack for the night and immediately went to sleep.

When the youngest Marine finally got back from the big party, he crawled into his rack around 01:00 in the pitch dark of the squad bay until his bare feet hit the greasy, cold turkey carcass between his sheets at the foot of his bed. Surprised, he jumped out of his rack, grabbed his bayonet and stabbed that cooked bird repeatedly until he finally identified it as a half-eaten turkey.

About that time, a Korean War veteran in the bottom bunk began laughing so hard that he could not defend himself as the 17-year old grabbed the turkey carcass by the neck hole and beat the veteran over his head as stuffing and turkey parts splattered all over the veteran's rack, the surrounding deck and several nearby racks. Yelling: "You did it. I know you did it" so loud that he woke up darned near everybody except

Eladio and I. We were both sleeping the deep slumber of the soused but pure at heart, so we missed the whole darned show.

The next morning, the young Marine's squad leader discovered that he had light-fingered a loaded .45-caliber pistol and gone AWOL (i.e., Absent Without Leave) into the night.

When that young Marine turned himself in about a month later, he was initially tossed into the brig. However, we were so short-handed during Christmas Running Guard (4 hours on duty, 8 off duty, 4 hours back on duty, 8 hours off duty, etc., etc. 24/7 for about four weeks to accommodate all of the returning Korean vets who went home for Christmas) that we could not afford to throw a highly-trained, competent MP into the brig. So we give him another loaded .45-caliber pistol and assigned him to be a prisoner chaser at the base brig that he had just bailed out of.

What goes around comes around.

41. THE PERFECT PRISONER

When Colonel Chesty Puller, the Commanding Officer of the 1st Marine Regiment, got the word that the 1st Marine Division was surrounded by three ChiCom divisions, Chesty's response was "Great, now we can shoot in any direction. Those bastards won't get away this time." Unfortunately, the U.S. Army Command, under extreme tactical pressure from the ChiComs, ordered their forces to retreat. So that's what they did, and in the process they left all sorts of heavy equipment like artillery guns, vehicles, heavy duty mobile generators and more than one field hospital which contained quite a few bed-ridden American soldiers.

A young Army corporal (I'll call him Bob because I have forgotten his name too), was among the many wounded soldiers left behind by the Army. The stress of that situation poisoned the well of Bob's attitude toward the U.S. Army more than somewhat, especially after he heard that the Chinese had killed all of the wounded soldiers at another Army field hospital, piled the bodys together, poured gasoline on them, and then burned the entire pile.

Fortunately for Bob, in their hard fought drive to the sea where the U.S. Navy and their 14-inch Naval cannons were waiting to defend them, the U.S. Marines decimated three ChiCom divisions, pummeled everything that the Chinese put in their way, and on the side rescued Bob and all of the other wounded soldiers in their abandoned field hospital. Not surprisingly, Cpl. Bob became very partial to the U.S. Marine Corps.

About 11 months later, Cpl. Bob went AWOL from a nearby Army base about two hours by car north of us, and returned to his home in San Jose where our Moffett SPs or MPs picked him up and brought him to my brig. You could not have a happier guy in the slammer. Bob was very glad to be there. He was with elements of the Marine unit that had saved him from Chinese firing squads, death by Chinese bayonet practice, or whatever horrible fate bedbound U.S. Army soldiers would have faced when captured during the weeks of fierce fighting near the Chosin reservoir.

Bob stayed with us about 10 days before two Army MPs came to get him. We were on running guard at that time, and the last thing I did on my watch was to turn Bob over to the Army MPs before I turned the brig over to Pfc. Joe Bolling. We all hated to see Bob go. He really brightened a somber military brig with his cheerful "can do" attitude.

Eight hours later when I returned to duty on running guard in the brig, there was Bob's smiling face looking out through the bars. What the heck? Initially, I thought that Bob and his escorts hadn't departed the base yet. Actually, while I was sleeping, Bob was returned to his home base a couple of hours north of Moffett, somehow went over the hill again, returned to San Jose again where our SPs or MPs picked him up again, and he was returned to the Moffett brig again; all in eight hours. We were glad to see him again, but not so soon.

That second and last time, the Army MPs showed up to get him after just two days. We all missed ol' Bob. That time the Army must have thrown away the key because we did not see Bob again. In fact, I kind of thought that I might see his smiling face and sunny disposition peeking through the bars again until the last day before I departed for Pensacola.

42. USMC INSPECTOR GENERAL

The Marine Detachment at NAS Moffett Field was scheduled to be inspected by the Inspector General for the entire U.S. Marine Corps. This was not a minor event, so we gave it our best shot for two whole days. Everything had to be squared-away with clean sweep/mop-downs fore and aft, and white glove pre-inspections galore so that even the brig was absolutely squared away.

MSgt O'Day was going to pre-inspect everything before the IG's inspection, so I knew that we needed some coffee in our large, new percolator. There was nothing like fresh coffee brewing to make the brig smell even more welcoming than usual. Yeah, that's right. However, I had never made coffee with that new percolator before, so I asked our six prisoners if anyone knew how to make a decent cup of coffee in it. One of our regular prisoners—he had good intentions but a lot of bad habits—said that he knew all about percolators and other good kitchen stuff like that, so I turned the task over to him.

What a mistake that was. That wayward sailor put in at least two times more coffee than needed, then threw in a whole freshly broken egg, shell and all, and cooked it a heck of a long time to saturate the brig with a strong coffee aroma.

That was the strongest coffee that I had ever tried to choke down. It was so strong that I wouldn't have been surprised if the sugar spoon would have stood up in the middle of my cup with no other support. It was bloody awful, and I told that prisoner that was the last batch of coffee that he would ever screw up in my brig.

In fact, I was just about to pour the whole pot down a potty when MSgt O'Day walked into the room, poured himself a cup of that gut wrenching brew, took a sip and, to my absolute surprise, he declared it the best darned coffee that he had drunk since World War II. He wasn't kidding. He poured himself a second cup and drank that too while he and I made the rounds throughout the entire brig.

Just then, we heard the Corporal of the Guard down the hall call all of the Marines down there to attention. The IG was coming our way, but after two days of serious cleaning, shining and painting, I felt pretty confident that we would pass that inspection. MSgt O'Day finished his coffee, put his cup back in a drawer out of sight, and looked down the hall to see where the IG was at that moment.

Long story short, the IG saw MSgt O'Day from a distance and yelled "O'Day, I haven't seen you since China." O'Day called out something of the same vintage, they met about 20 feet down the hall from the brig, shook hands warmly, turned around and headed back to O'Day's office to swap sea stories and drink some more coffee.

The IG of the whole U.S. Marine Corps never did inspect our brig, and our six prisoners at that time did not quit gripping about our two days of cleaning, shining, painting and squaring away the whole area all for naught. What the heck, like my dear old dad often said: "Anything worth doing is worth doing well." I was just darned happy that I didn't get gigged by the IG after all of that extra work. But one thing is for sure, if we had flunked that inspection, it would have been a month of Sundays before Joe D. and I would have even been considered for promotion to corporal.

43. POLICE UP THE BRASS

That story about our IG inspection reminded me in a convoluted manner about a ten-cent movie we saw at the base theater. The audience was probably half Navy and half Marines one night when the feature movie was an old 1939 tear jerker about a poor, pitiful, helpless little lady played, I believe, by Joan Crawford (yuck!). Anyway, the story was about how poor Joanie had been horribly mistreated by some nasty S.O.B. for most of the movie. But then, finally, when she could take no more abuse, she picked up the bad guy's pistol and emptied it into him up close and very personal. Good for her.

However, since this was a B.S. Hollywood movie, she immediately went into the deepest, darkest depths of theatrical remorse, and cried out ever so pitifully: "Oh my God, what shall I do?" Immediately, about half of the packed house responded in unison and in their best Range Master voices with: "Police up the brass and move back to the 500-yard line."

44. PFC. SNYDER

Pfc. Snyder was the shortest Marine I ever saw. When his bayonet was attached at the muzzle of his M1 rifle, that combined length gave the impression that it was taller than the Marine carrying it. With his heavily creased, always smiling face of a second-generation Australian aborigine, this proven combat veteran was always quietly watching and learning in the background. He seldom said much and never caused any trouble until one night in town at a party when a giant of a black man got mad at him and tried to crush the little fellow with a bear hug. Later, when I asked what happened, Snyder simply explained that: "I felt like I was going to pass out, so I took out my knife and I cut him."

Cpl. Hooker, who was also at that party, told me that Snyder's assailant had something like 350 stitches in his stomach and other parts before the doctors had finally sewed him back together again. That big civilian would be eating his meals through a straw for a heck of a long time. As Cpl. Hooker mimicked Pfc. Snyder, he said: "I cut him long…wide…deep…frequent and continuously. I stuck it in him once and I walked around him twice. I cut that sum'bitch up real good…and I'd do it again."

After that, I never doubted for one minute that this quiet little Marine warrior would do the same danged thing again if threatened. Which reminds me again about Mr. Cowboy back in El Dorado, Kansas, who told me that the important thing wasn't the size of the dog in the fight, it was the size of the fight in the dog.

Do I hear an "Aaaaa-men"?

45. MEMORABLE MOMENTS

In late November, one of our Navy aviators at NAS Moffett Field committed suicide by diving his F8F jet fighter from high altitude straight down into a wooded hill on the back 40 acres of Stanford University. The crash burned up a lot of trees and undergrowth, and there were little bitty, gory body parts and airplane wreckage scattered randomly all over the area. For a short time, that crash site was like a scaled down Dante's "Inferno."

As a member of the armed USMC MP Security detail that accompanied the crash crew from Moffett Field, I watched a Navy Corpsman friend pick a burned finger out of a bush and bag it. I remember how he stared at that gruesome member for a long time, maybe a minute or so, as if lost in thought. Then he looked at me solemnly, and asked me confidentially if I was sure that I still wanted to be a Navy/Marine fighter pilot.

I had to admit that at that moment, with my lunch about to become a high order barf, the issue was indeed somewhat in doubt.

46 "THAT'S MEN'S WORK"

Pfc. Eladio "Gunny" Gonzales, my actual blood brother (I still have the scar on the heal of my right hand to prove our mixing of our blood) and veteran of more than a year on line in the Korean War with Colonel Ray Murray's 5th Marine Brigade, was as cool under stress as anyone I have ever known. However, one night while on MP motor patrol duty outside the base perimeter, the Corporal of the Guard called us to say that a farmer demanded that we run off "some sailors making whoopee" in a car on the farmer's adjacent property. In accordance with our Standard Operating Procedures (SOPs), Eladio and I drove up to the parked car slowly, our lights on bright as we made as much noise as possible to alert the parked lovers that the party was over and it was time to get squared away and move along. That had always worked well, but this time we saw no indication that the couple inside the car even knew that we were there.

Finally, Eladio slowly got out of the truck, slammed the door a couple of times extra loud to get their attention, flashed his light in the car's back seat, and went berserk. Surprisingly, nothing happened inside that car. Finally, Eladio banged on the roof of the car with his billy club and demanded that the two sailors get the hell out of that car immediately if not sooner.

To my absolute surprise, out popped the two best-looking Waves at NAS Moffett Field. One was the Base Commander's cute little blond secretary who I am sure was lusted after by every mother's son on the base. The other Wave worked in the Pass and Tag Office next to our main gate. She was so pretty that darned near every guy who saw her eee-mediately fell in lust with her, and usually found a bunch of reasons to visit the Pass and Tag Office as often as possible to do whatever business that they could conjure up to be there.

The big joke was that I had never approached either one of them because I figured that they probably thought that they were too special for enlisted guys, or at least their tastes were too rich for enlisted guys who were not receiving flight skins (i.e., extra pay for flying), so they only dated unmarried pilots who were paid a lot more money and could keep the good times rolling.

Mutually bent out of shape—I had never been in that situation before—we finally decided that we had to take those two gals back to the base and book them with the Officer of the Day at the Navy SP office. That was our one and only MP arrest for anything like that although we had told scores of enlisted Marines, sailors and their gal pals to shape up and move-along under somewhat similar conditions. However, we never arrested anyone else for that kind of fooling around. Somehow, it did not seem right to arrest anyone for doing something that I wished I was doing.

Later, I asked Eladio why he became so P.O.ed with those women, since he was normally so darned cool. Eladio explained with an intentionally exaggerated, theatrically thick Mexican accent that he often affected for emphasis. He told me, quote: "Those women were doin' men's work."

Incidentally, neither Wave was ever formally disciplined to our knowledge, because neither Eladio nor I was ever called to testify at a hearing as the arresting MPs. Without our testimony, that was "Case Closed." Once again, youth and beauty had overcome darned near every related regulation in the U.S. Navy's extended library. Who'da thunk it before then? Not me.

47. CHESTY PULLER'S JEEP DRIVER

Colonel Chesty Puller's driver in Korea, Sgt. Orville Jones, was waiting at NAS Moffett Field for reassignment. Sgt. Jones had a bunk on the exact opposite side of the 100-bed squad bay from me, and he kept to himself so I didn't bump into him very often. I never stood duty with him and seldom had more than a nodding acquaintance with him. He was a fairly quiet guy who didn't say much, but when asked a direct question, he would give a straight answer.

Every once in a while, some difference of opinion would come up about Colonel, later Major General Chesty Puller, a Marine icon and the commander of the 1st Marine Regiment of the 1st Marine Division during the historic battles at the Inchon invasion, the first and second battles for Seoul, the "frozen Chosin Reservoir" campaign along the line of attack from Koto-ri to Hungnam North Korea and the American fleet, and the many battles to establish and sustain the DMZ at the 38th parallel.

One evening in December, 1953 while on Running Guard, a group of us grunts were talking about a post-Chosin reservoir battle where the ChiComs held the high ground and elements of the 1st Marines Regiment were ordered to remove them mui pronto. Despite artillery and air support, the Marines were repelled twice by a well dug-in Chinese reinforced company who were determined to keep possession of that tactically significant high ground. According to Sgt. Jones, when he and Chesty arrived in his jeep, the assaulting Marines were regrouping and preparing for a third assault.

Chesty asked a sergeant how many ChiComs were up there, and the weary warrior reported "Many, many, Sir." Then a second sergeant reported essentially the same thing when asked. Finally, Chesty asked a Gunny Sergeant who he had known during WWII, who reported "There's a whole shit pot full of those bastards up there, Sir." Chesty smiled and said: "Finally, I've found someone who knows how to count."

Chesty met with his company commanders to clarify that tactical problem and assess the situation. Then he picked up a spare Browning Automatic Rifle (BAR), slung an ammunition bandolier over his shoulder, yelled "Follow me," and began walking up that hill while firing at targets of opportunity. The battle weary Marines picked up their weapons and followed Chesty up that hill, and after a pitched battle, they took that high ground to win a hard-fought victory.

FYI: another difference between the Marines and the U.S. Army is that the Marine officers' command is "Follow me," because they lead from the front. By contrast, the Army officers' command is "Charge," and then too often they observe from the rear with the gear. That could explain the average Marine grunts' much higher opinion of their officers.

The best story verified by Sgt. Orville Jones, was about General McArthur's visit soon after the Marines had landed at Inchon, captured Seoul, turned the capital city of several million people over to the U.S. Army, and then the Army almost lost Seoul back to the North Koreans. Chesty could not afford to have the enemy behind him, so several Marine battalions had to go back to recapture that war-torn city in a nasty house-by-house, eyeball-to-eyeball campaign. Most U.S. civilians have not heard about that epic second battle for Seoul. I wonder why.

As you may recall, there was no love lost between McArthur and the Marines going back to WWII in the Pacific Ocean. The following Marine ditty originated during the battle for Guadalcanal where the Marines stopped the Japanese previously successful surge to win the Pacific Theater.

> "They wanted the Army to go to Tulagi,
> But Dugout Doug said 'No'.
> It isn't the season, besides there's a reason.
> They ain't got no USO."

In fact, McArthur had initially turned down Marine support in Korea until the American and South Korean Armies were pushed back to the Pusan Perimeter, and in danger of being overrun or pushed into the ocean by North Korean armored units. McArthur finally agreed to have a Marine regimental fire team join in the Pusan fight. After the Marines arrived, we refused to be pushed back, we stopped the North Korean surge and changed the whole tactical situation. Soon after that, the newly arrived 1st Marine Division landed at Inchon, which threatened to cut off the North Korean Army still massed further down the Korean peninsula around the Pusan Perimeter.

After the North Korean's double defeat by the Marines at Seoul, the Marines again began their offensive northward while the re-energized, newly reinforced U.S. Army and South Korean Armies moved up the east coast and central sectors against the then out-maneuvered North Koreans.

At that time, with victory suddenly a strong probability in some military minds, General McArthur took the opportunity to visit Korea from his headquarters in Japan for some on-the-spot senior command meetings and a lot of Kodak moments. Colonel Chesty Puller was assigned to give General McArthur a tactical assessment of the war in the field on the west coast of Korea. So Chesty, his driver Sgt. Orville Jones, McArthur and his entourage drove north of Seoul and stopped on a prominent hill top.

After they had all gotten out of their Jeeps and were looking around for the best photographic angles, McArthur asked Chesty where the Marine forces were located. Chesty pointed back and casually said that the Marines were behind them not too far. Then McArthur asked Chesty where the North Korean army was. Chesty told McArthur quite calmly that the enemy was just over the hill a short distance straight ahead.

McArthur scrambled into Chesty's lead jeep and bellowed at Chesty and Sgt. Jones: "GET ME OUT OF HERE!" Sgt. Jones said that he was driving pretty darned fast for a jeep on rough terrain, but McArthur wanted him to drive a lot faster until they were safely within the Marine MLR forward positions. However, when McArthur got back to Japan, he wrote on 21 September 1950: "I have just returned from visiting the Marines at the front, and there is not a finer fighting organization in the world." Later he was heard to say: "If I had one more division like the 1st Marine Division, I could win this war." Finally, Dugout Doug got it right.

48. SURPRISE, SURPRISE

Soon after the F8F fighter plane crashed at Stanford University, I wrote another letter home asking for yet another box of Mom's extra special chocolate chip cookies and another whimsically illustrated letter from Dad. That was pretty nervy of me after she had sent a cubic-foot size box of her special chocolate chip cookies only a few weeks earlier. When I received the latest box at mail call, I stuffed a few cookies in the hand-grenade pocket of my battle jacket, posted Dad's latest illustrated letter on the bulletin board for all to enjoy, then I got out of the way. I think every Marine present grabbed at least one of Mom's justly famous cookies. Thank goodness Mom responded because my blood/chocolate-chip cookie level was getting very low again.

As Pfc. Joe Bolling and I were heading for the gym for basketball practice, Sgt. Brightman told me to hustle on over to the Marine personnel office muy pronto. Naturally, I figured that I had received my orders to Pensacola. But in that case, why weren't Joe Bolling, George Bailey and Bill Crowley called over there too? For a guy who was too often working without a net, I had gotten to the place where I really disliked surprises involving my near future duty or lack thereof.

When I reported to the personnel office, my mind was racing. Did it have something to do with the accidental misfire in the brig? Did somebody spill the beans about our Marine Corps Birthday escapades? Had the local Police Department filed a complaint about Cpl. Bessier and I playing silly games with their police officers (when the shoe was on the other foot)? Had "Sea Daddy's" midnight three-star VIP gotten huffy? How about those two beautiful dyke waves we arrested?

As soon as I arrived at the office, MSgt O'Day put down his cup of coffee, poured me a cup of coffee with sugar and cream just the way I once liked it, shook my hand and congratulated me for making Corporal in less than 12 months. The average time in service for promotion from Private First Class to Corporal was about 18 months, but I would be in Pensacola long before that so somebody, probably the colonel, must have greased the skids. I guess there really is a "fast track" when somebody at the top of the chain of command wants to make a point.

Isn't it grand how time flies when you are having fun?

49. THE NAKED TRUTH

One night on the midnight to 04:00 watch, a car full of soused sailors pulled up to the main gate. My partner and I were fully occupied with sorting out who was who when a second car pulled up right behind the Navy merry makers' mobile party. Since I had just checked the last sailor on the right side of that first car, when the first car continued into the base, I was still on the passenger side of the second car when he pulled up. At a glance, I noticed that the young driver was apparently wearing a Navy officer's dress uniform, and his lovely companion was apparently wearing a very low-cut strapless evening gown.

Rather than hold the officer longer than necessary while I walked around to the driver's side of his car, I stuck my head into the front right seat window so that I could read the officer's ID as quickly as possible. However, something pulled my eyes down to the young lady's chest. That's when I realized that the young lady was not wearing a strapless evening gown after all. In fact, she was not wearing anything at all that I could see. She was buck naked from her toes to her top knot, absolutely motionless and totally mute as I turned my head so that she and I were awkwardly nose to nose.

My mind raced as I tried to remember if there was a Special Order that newly minted Cpl. Dave Ferman should interfere with any drop-dead gorgeous young naked lady by keeping her from entering NAS Moffett Field with some Navy flyboy at 02:17 in the morning.

Since I could not remember anything like that at the spur of the moment, and did not want to bother the Officer of the Day with trifles, I checked the young officer's ID and windshield sticker, stepped back from his car, saluted smartly, and waved the young officer and his lovely lady friend through the gate. I would have hated to be a party pooper.

Besides, like I said before, I was not going to hassle that young warrior for doing something that I would be glad to be doing if the tables were turned around.

Go Navy.

50. THAT #$%&(@)+!! LENNY

One of our so-called elite group of 12 enlisted pilot candidates—that "elite" hogwash always made me laugh, but several of our guys really ate it up—was from a wealthy family. I'll call him Lenny rather than his given name since in this age of litigation, his lawyer is probably a junk yard dog and I don't need the bother. Anyway, Lenny had somehow tricked a physically blessed, incredibly stacked, but apparently not too bright young lady into believing that she and Lenny were legally married. However, I understand that they were not really married because Lenny used a phony ID when they were married during an all-night party in Reno, Nevada one weekend a couple of months before.

Somehow, this gal didn't know about that slicky boy scam and neither did most of the rest of us; me included. However, after a couple of months of happy brown-bagging together, Lenny must have gotten tired of that arrangement. The honeymoon was over, but the young lady did not have a clue about what was happening. Somehow Lenny had sent his "wife" an official Government Speed Letter—forging government documents is a major "No No" that is punishable by many moons of making little rocks out of big rocks—which said that he was killed on a secret mission overseas.

A too-slick-by-half character who too often cut too many corners to get his nefarious way, Lenny probably figured that letter would get rid of her post haste if not sooner, and she would probably get over it fairly soon and then move on. After all, she did not know Lenny's real name, so what could she do about that?

Well, for one thing, she could show up at the main gate at NAS Moffett Field to collect the widow's benefits that she believed the government owed her. However, none of us Marines recognized Lenny's fake name so initially we weren't much help for her. But, unfortunately for Lenny, every one of us recognized his customized chopped, channeled and supercharged 1953 Ford coupe that she described in quite a bit of detail. That car was a classic, a car to be cherished, one of a kind; so Lenny's name was Mudd.

The next day, I was standing guard on the main gate when one of our wounded Marines, Cpl. Sanchez I believe, began feeling really rotten and needed relief eee-mediately if not sooner. So I called the Corporal of the Guard and told him that Sanchez needed to be relieved right away. However, when the motor patrol truck arrived at the gate, the replacement guard was coming to relieve me and not Sanchez. Say what?

When I arrived at the C.O.'s office in the Marine Administration building, the tight jawed, humorless guy sitting at the C.O.'s desk was an FBI agent who was wearing a still-buttoned Dick Tracy overcoat; indoors no less. I kid you not. He really looked like comic book dress-up time, and I nearly laughed in his face until he took all of the Ha Ha out of the occasion by announcing right at the beginning that "Anything you say may be used against you." Holy mackerel, what a revolting development that was.

When questioned individually about Lenny's whereabouts by that FBI guy, Pfc. George Bailey (later Col. George Bailey), Pfc. Joe Bolling (later Lt. Col. Joe Bolling), Bill Crowley, several other Marines and I all pleaded ignorance. However, as soon as the multiple séances with the FBI guy were over, somebody drove off base and called Lenny at his high school sweetheart's sorority house at the University of Oregon, and told him that he'd better run for the border, or else get a heck of a good lawyer and turn himself in mui pronto.

Later, George filled me in on what happened, but the guy who called Lenny in Oregon could have been any one of a half of a dozen other Marines also. That guy sure as heck was not me. I had no idea where Lenny was and did not give a flip about his off-base antics or whereabouts anyway. I didn't have a clue where he was on extended leave, and did not give a flip anyway. Lenny was not one of my favorite people; not by a long shot.

About a week later, Lenny, his ultra-rich mama and her bulldog corporate lawyer showed up at the main gate, and Lenny immediately found himself inside the base brig looking out through the bars. Ironically, he had served as a prisoner chaser at that brig only a couple of weeks earlier. At least, he needed no orientation in the brig.

The next day, I received my orders to report for flight training at the Pensacola Flight Training Command. Amazingly, they gave me 30 days of travel time and apparently unearned vacation time between NAS Moffett Field in northern California and Pensacola, Florida when I could have flown by commercial airliner to Pensacola in one day, or for darn sure, two days at the most. That was kind of a mystery that I could not understand. I wondered why in the dickens was I given all of that travel time and unearned vacation leave while Pfc.'s George Bailey, Joe Bowling and Bill Crowley were still back at NAS Moffett Field waiting their travel orders for what turned out to be several more weeks?

But like my dear old Dad often said: "Never look a gift horse in the mouth." So once again, I saluted smartly, packed my sea bag, and danced out of the barracks door. Later I learned that my C.O. probably did that to get me far away from Lenny's bulldog lawyer. Thank you colonel.

51. SGT. BENNY

As I was finally checking out to go to Pensacola for flight training, I stopped by to say goodbye to a fine, devoted and loyal four-footed friend. Sgt. Benny was our unit mascot bulldog that looked just exactly like the official Marine mascot in national Marine advertisements. He had worn his three stripes on his red and gold harness with obvious pride. You will seldom see a flat-out strutting swagger until you have seen Sgt. Benny from the rear while he was marching on the drill field behind one of our units. He just knew that he was a very important bulldog, and he showed his pride by his strutting walk.

Sgt. Benny had been inducted into the Marine Corps in 1953 when the 5th Marines returned to the United States. After indoctrination and all of his shots, he was processed through a Marine doggy boot camp that was as close to the real thing as could be done with a bulldog. If Sgt. Benny had been blessed with thumbs, his boot camp would have been even more authentic.

After doggie boot camp, Pfc. Benny served with honor and distinction in base security, which was his Military Occupational Specialty (MOS), and had been promoted to Cpl. Benny after serving for 18 doggie months (three and a half people months), and then to buck sergeant after 18 more doggie months. His training and accomplishments were carefully recorded in his DD-214 file in the base Personnel Office. Unfortunately, Sgt. Benny got into a tussle with the new base commander's mangy mutt, and had bitten its fat butt several times during the base Change of Command ceremony described before. For that, Sgt. Benny was busted down to Pfc. Benny and served about a week in and around the base brig with only a few potty breaks each day. Nevertheless, Pfc. Benny was a good Marine, and would undoubtedly regain one of his lost stripes after 18 more doggie months if he could just stay away from those dastardly interloping Navy K-nines who had no business lifting a leg or pooping on Pfc. Benny's very own parade ground. Pfc. Benny always did his business on the grass. Semper fi.

52. SGT. RECKLESS

Remembering Sgt. Benny reminds me of a donkey sized Mongolian mare that was bought by a Marine officer in Korea to carry cargo to the front lines from the distant assembly point for gear in the rear, and to bring back wounded Marines from the Navy Corpsmen on the line to the forward aid stations. To look at her, she was a quiet, docile little mare with no particular distinguishing physical indications of her staunch dedication to her assigned duties.

Sgt. Reckless performed her duties carrying recoilless rifles and their ammunition up into the hills where the 5th Marines were dueling at close quarters with the Chinese version of our recoilless rifles as well as a whole potful of mortars. The fighting was fierce, but she never flinched despite the intensity of the battles and the almost continuous explosions on the trail and at the front lines. Sgt. Reckless was lightly wounded twice, but she never hesitated to continue her assignment to bring up ammo and launchers to the Marine MLR (i.e., Main Line of Resistance), and take walking-wounded Marines back down the hills away from the battle areas.

The fascinating part of the story is that Sgt. Reckless performed her duties entirely solo. She did it all on her own. She dropped off wounded Marines at the aid station, walked over to the ammo depot where she was loaded down with recoilless rifles, ammo, and other essentials, then turned around and delivered her load to the hard pressed Marines on the MLR where battles were raging and Chinese counter-battery artillery fire was intense. Sgt. Reckless never flinched.

After the Cease Fire was finally signed and the 5th Marines returned to the United States, Sgt. Reckless lived out the rest of her life in peace and relative quiet at USMC Camp Pendleton, California. But she was remembered by all of those veterans of the 5th Marines, and a couple of Commandants of the Marine Corps who visited her in her comfortable stables and lush pasture. There is something about the Marine Corps that just seems to mesh with volunteer warriors, NCO bull dogs, and a truly heroic Mongolian mare.

53. COUSIN AMY HAD HER DOUBTS

While flying by commercial airliner from San Francisco to Denver on the way to flight school at Pensacola, a very pretty stewardess asked me if I would be so kind as to move to the back of the plane and hold one of two cute little babies that were being taken to New York City by one very haggard looking nanny. Who could resist a cutie pie like that; or the baby either?

All went well and the baby and I were bonding and cooing back and forth when the stewardess warned me that we could experience a big bump as the plane would begin its descent as it passed over the Front Range of the Rocky Mountains. Those words were barely out of her mouth when we hit a couple of tummy twisting bumps in the air, and the baby immediately barfed all over my green USMC winter service uniform.

I swear that little bitty baby upchucked a big load of barf all over my shirt, tie, trousers and jacket that the stewardess and I could not clean with a box of wiping cloths and a couple of damp airline towels. But she and I gave it our best shot because the smell was over-danged-whelming in the crowded cabin. Of course, my clean uniforms were stowed in my sea bag in the belly of the airliner and I could not get anything from them until I picked up my sea bag at the luggage carousel inside the Denver International Airport building.

That was my story when I was the last one to get off the airplane as my little cousin Amy waited my arrival on the tarmac at Denver. Of course, as a senior nursing student by that time, Amy did not believe the puking baby story no matter what I said. After all, no puking babies had deplaned in Denver. Of course not; they were sleeping angelically in fresh "footie" pajamas in their travel cribs with their exhausted nanny still onboard the airliner. Therefore, during my three-day stopover in Denver to finally meet Cousin Amy's lovely blond roommate in their mutual nursing class, Amy repeatedly asked me if I was sure that I really wanted to be an airplane driver.

Like my good buddy Pfc. (later Lt.Colonel) Joe D. Bolling often said: "Don't ask me no hard questions."

54. SWEATING BULLETS

After I had been home for about a week, George Bailey called from Moffett Field to tell me that after I cut out for Pensacola by that roundabout, leisurely route, that lying stinker Lenny "confessed" that I was the guy who wrote the Government Speed Letter for him, and I was the guy who should be in the slammer rather than Lenny. After all, Lenny testified that darned near all of the Marines at NAS Moffett Field knew that I had helped many of those heroic warriors write love letters to their wives and girlfriends because they weren't very good at that; and by their requests, I also helped them by occasionally drafting or editing their English grammar within their letters to family and friends. I was their unofficial English grammar tutor when I held chalk talks about nouns, verbs, adjectives, etc. in one of our classrooms. Heck, I was glad to be able to do that for those Marines who fought and won the most incredible combat campaign in the history of warfare under the most difficult terrain and subzero weather conditions imaginable. These were the men of the 1st, 5th and 7th Marine Brigades of the 1st Marine Division who had inspired me to join the Marine Corps when I did. I was proud to be able to help them in any way that I could.

However, there is a heck of a huge difference between helping some English-grammar-challenged Marine warriors to compose letters to Mom and Pop back home and writing unauthorized Government Speed Letters to defraud a previously deceived wife. Fortunately, our Commanding Officer did not buy into Lenny's pack of raw horse manure, and eventually his general court martial sent Lenny to the Slammer for five years of hard labor, and I finally quit sweating bullets whenever I received a phone call from NAS Moffett Field.

55. HARD TIME WAS NOT THAT HARD

But the story did not end there. While we were in flight training, NavCad George Bailey heard from someone back at NAS Moffett Field that Lenny was then representing the Marine Detention Center—or whatever the heck it is called—in inter-service golf tournaments, and he was playing 18 holes most days with the base Commanding Officer, who was a golf addict. Then, a couple of years later, George Bailey heard that Lenny was released for good behavior on the golf course, and dishonorably discharged to return home to wallow in the lap of luxury in his rich mama's corporate paradise.

Like a wise man who would later be a full-bull colonel in my Marine Corps once said to me: "Behind every free spirit is a big, fat trust fund."

56. A TOAST BY THE USMC COMMANDANT

"The wonderful love of a beautiful maid,
The love of a staunch true man,
The love of a baby, unafraid,
Have existed since time began.

"But the greatest of loves,
The quintessence of loves,
Even greater than that of a mother,
Is the tender, passionate, infinite love,
Of one drunken Marine for another."

"Semper Fi."

General Louis H. Wilson, Commandant USMC, 10 Nov. 1978

57. PREAMBLE

I swear on a stack of bibles yeah high that if I had known what was waiting for me at Pensacola, I would have excused myself from Brigadier General Chesty Puller's entire experiment, returned to MCRD San Diego, reported to M.Sgt Ramsey, and squandered the rest of my enlistment as a junior DI and the senior kicker on the base football team. I kid you not.

APPENDIX

PREPARING FOR MARINE BOOT CAMP

To those who wish to be a part of the world's finest fighting force, my best advice to you is to begin running if you are not already seriously running for distance and your best time. If you want to not only survive Marine boot camp but thrive, you should be able to run at least five miles at a steady but fairly fast pace without stopping. If you can't do that, I suggest that you put off enlisting until you can run at least five miles with ease.

The second most important aspect is to work like the dickens on your IQ testing before you enlist so that you will get the best score that you are capable of getting the one time when it really counts. The IQ test is tricky, and I dare say that darn few score as well on his/her first IQ test as they would score on their second or third IQ test. The problem here is that almost all young Marines are only tested once for their permanent record, so they need to take that test several times before enlisting to get fully oriented and comfortable with that test. The fact remains; the higher your IQ score, the more normally closed doors will be open to you.

A 100 score is normal, but a 120 score is needed for Officer Candidate School (OCS), Drill Instructor School, various technical schools and timely promotions. A 140 score or above qualifies you for

Mensa and, all things being equal, that will open darned near every door in the Marine Corps if you are healthy and have a good attitude.

A word to the wise; you may be partial to, and even proud of your tattoos, but in the U.S. Marine Corps, no tattoos are allowed that are visible when wearing short trousers or a short-sleeved shirt. Even then, the content of any visible tattoo can disqualify you. If you have tattoos on your head or face, don't even think about joining the U.S. Marine Corps.

A few thoughts about IQ tests in the U.S. Marine Corps will definitely be beneficial; i.e., the higher your IQ score, the better for your first tour of duty in the Marines. Case in point; my first IQ test was taken at the USMC recruiting office in Wichita, Kansas while I was waiting for my broken hand to heal so I could enlist with a group of hot-to-trot guys from my home town. I did okay, scoring above 120 which was the qualifying score for a potential officer candidate. Those lucky guesses opened a few otherwise closed doors.

On the second IQ test, I took in boot camp to verify my first IQ test back in Wichita. At that time, I was a bit better oriented so I was a bit more comfortable, and I scored 8 points higher than the first test. How did that happen?

I had learned a lot about timed tests from the recruiter's IQ test: i.e., it's always best to answer all of the easy questions as fast as possible, then go back and wrestle with the more difficult questions in whatever the time remaining. On my second IQ test, I saved the hardest questions for last so that I timed out with only a few of the harder questions unanswered. Too many recruits waste valuable time concentrating on the hardest questions in strict rotation, so they don't have sufficient time remaining to answer a bunch of easier questions that would have raised their score,

My third IQ test in 1953 was specifically required for acceptance at flight school at Pensacola, Florida. Comfortable with the process and primed from my prior notes, I had another improvement on my IQ test and received a Mensa-qualification score although I didn't feel any smarter than after the first IQ test back in Wichita. That opened darned near all of the doors that had been previously closed, and even seemed to overlook a few of my minor faux pas as well.

In some ways, IQ tests are much like crossword puzzles in the newspapers. Just because someone can fill a lot of the same blank squares time after time by rote does not mean that he or she is really smart. The IQ test is much more challenging. So do yourself a favor and take a few IQ tests (at least more than one IQ test) before enlisting in the U.S. Marine Corps. During your first test or tests, try to remember as many of the harder questions as you can, check them out after each test, and when you finally take the IQ test that counts for your Marine record evermore; you will be glad that you did.

Semper fi. Gung ho. Ooooo-raaah.

www.ingramcontent.com/pod-product-compliance
Lightning Source LLC
LaVergne TN
LVHW091549060526
838200LV00036B/764